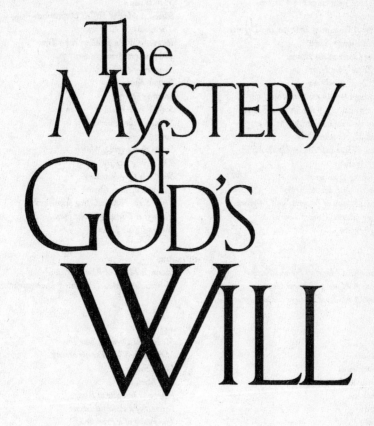

The MYSTERY of GOD'S WILL

Publications by Charles R. Swindoll

BOOKS

Active Spirituality

The Bride

Come Before Winter

Compassion: Showing We Care in a Careless World

David: A Man of Passion and Destiny

Dear Graduate

Dropping Your Guard

Encourage Me

Esther: A Woman of Strength and Dignity

The Finishing Touch

Flying Closer to the Flame

For Those Who Hurt

The Grace Awakening

Growing Deep in the Christian Life

Growing Strong in the Seasons of Life

Growing Wise in Family Life

Hand Me Another Brick

Home: Where Life Makes Up Its Mind

Hope Again

Improving Your Serve

Intimacy with the Almighty

Joseph: A Man of Integrity and Forgiveness

Killing Giants, Pulling Thorns

Laugh Again

Leadership: Influence That Inspires

Living Above the Level of Mediocrity

Living Beyond the Daily Grind, Books I and II

The Living Insights Study Bible—General Editor

Living on the Ragged Edge

Make Up Your Mind

Man to Man

Moses: A Man of Selfless Dedication

The Quest for Character

Recovery: When Healing Takes Time

The Road to Armageddon

Sanctity of Life

Simple Faith

Starting Over

Start Where You Are

Strengthening Your Grip

Stress Fractures

Strike the Original Match

The Strong Family

Suddenly One Morning

Tale of the Tardy Oxcart

Three Steps Forward, Two Steps Back

Victory: A Winning Game Plan for Life

You and Your Child

MINIBOOKS

Abraham: A Model of Pioneer Faith

David: A Model of Pioneer Courage

Esther: A Model of Pioneer Independence

Moses: A Model of Pioneer Vision

Nehemiah: A Model of Pioneer Determination

BOOKLETS

Anger

Attitudes

Commitment

Dealing with Defiance

Demonism

Destiny

Divorce

Eternal Security

Forgiving and Forgetting

Fun Is Contagious!

God's Will

Hope

Impossibilities

Integrity

Intimacy with the Almighty

Leisure

The Lonely Whine of the Top Dog

Make Your Dream Come True

Making the Weak Family Strong

Moral Purity

Our Mediator

Peace . . . in Spite of Panic

Portrait of a Faithful Father

The Power of a Promise

Prayer

Reflections from the Heart—A Prayer Journal

Seeking the Shepherd's Heart—A Prayer Journal

Sensuality

Stress

This is No Time for Wimps

Tongues

When Your Comfort Zone Gets the Squeeze

Woman

CHARLES R. SWINDOLL

The MYSTERY of GOD'S WILL

What Does He Want For Me?

WORD PUBLISHING

NASHVILLE

A Thomas Nelson Company

THE MYSTERY OF GOD'S WILL
by Charles R. Swindoll

Copyright © 1999 by Charles R. Swindoll, Inc.

Published by Word Publishing, a Thomas Nelson Company,
P. O. Box 141000, Nashville, Tennessee 37214.

Unless otherwise indicated, Scripture quotations used in this book are from the
New American Standard Bible (NASB) © 1960, 1962, 1963, 1971, 1972, 1973, 1975,
1977 by the Lockman Foundation. Used by permission.

ISBN 0-8499-1133-8

Printed in the United States of America

Dedication

~

These recent years have been marked by
times of uncertainty and mystery
for my wife and me.

God has seemed a paradox in many ways
as we have continued to seek His will
and walk in obedience to His Word.

He has sometimes been so close
we could almost feel the flapping of angels' wings
as they hovered around His throne . . .
but at other times, He has seemed so distant
we felt strangely confused, even abandoned.

Those are not easy waters for a Christian couple to navigate,
especially when you feel you are journeying
without answers and lacking reassurance.

Two couples have meant the most to us
during these turbulent, soul-searching months:

DAVID AND WENDY CHAVANNE

and

JOHNNY AND CASEY KOONS

Because of the love they have demonstrated to us
through their loyal friendship, encouraging words,
compassionate acts of mercy, and intercessory support,
I gratefully and affectionately dedicate this book to them.

Contents

❧

Introduction

◆

All deep earnest thinking is but the intrepid effort of the soul
to keep the open independence of her sea, while
the wildest winds of Heaven and earth conspire to
cast her on the treacherous, slavish shore.

—HERMAN MELVILLE, *Moby Dick*

So MUCH OF THE CONFUSION we encounter in life goes back to our not understanding God and how He does His inscrutable work in our lives. In recent years, I have struggled with many of what I am calling "mysteries" in my own life. As a result, I have come to a new understanding of God's will. In the past, I often viewed the Christian life, or even just life in general, as a matter of getting from here to there . . . from point A to point B. I now believe that God's will for us in this life is not some black-and-white objective equation designed to take us to an appointed destination here on earth as much as it is about the journey itself. It is not so much about our own well-thought-through "mission" for our lives as it is about what matters to Him in our lives.

Our human tendency is to focus solely on our calling—on where we should go, how we should get there, and what exactly we should do about it. God's concern is the process that He is taking us through to mature us and ready us, making us more like His Son. In other words, all of us—including *you*—are works in process.

Think of the men and women in Scripture who were made aware of their calling from the Lord, but who soon discovered that carrying out that call or arriving at that place of service was extremely convoluted, often surprising, and occasionally downright painful. In fact, sometimes they didn't get "there" at all, at least not where they had expected to go.

Abraham was told to sacrifice his son Isaac. That was to be his mission, clearly stated and plainly communicated by the Lord. But in the final analysis, God was testing him, all the time having other plans in mind. Surprising to Abraham? Yes. Mysterious? Absolutely.

David was anointed to become king of Israel. That was the stated goal. Samuel said so. But within a short time, David became the object of King Saul's jealousy and wrath. And for a dozen or more years, the pressure he endured mounted to such an extent that David must have wondered if he would ever even live to see his day on the throne. Unexpected by David? Certainly.

And what about poor Hosea? What a scandal his life was. Yet it was the Lord's will that Hosea marry the adulterous Gomer, taking her back after her continued unfaithfulness. Another mystery . . . from our point of view.

Then there was Joseph, maligned, mistreated, and falsely accused. How could that possibly be God's will for one of His chosen vessels, seemingly called by God to be a great leader? Well, it was.

Or consider John the Baptizer, who was beheaded at the whim of Herod's stepdaughter. Talk about mysterious! How in the world could that be the will of God for one He loved much and had used so mightily?

And Paul. After being so clearly called by God as the apostle to the Gentiles, he spent the balance of his life jumping from one frying pan into another fire. How did God's will work in his reaching that goal? Painful. Full of obstacles. Interrupted. Mysterious!

The list would go on endlessly if we were to recount all the mysterious ways of God's will and work in the lives of His people down through the centuries.

It is these mysterious, surprising, and, yes, often distressing aspects of God's will that I intend to address in the following pages. For some reason, I don't find much written on the subject. Far more often I read of how clearly and calmly the Lord takes His people from here to there, with little struggle and almost no doubt. It's quick, simple, and easy . . . or so I'm told.

Because that has not been my experience, and because I rarely find it modeled in the Scriptures or in people's lives today, it seemed appropriate that the mysterious, vague, and disturbing side of obedience be acknowledged. There is no harm in not being able to explain why or in admitting that followers of Christ are frequently at a loss to find human logic in the path He designs for us to walk. If nothing else, I hope this book will give you permission to confess, "This is beyond my ability to understand. It's a mystery."

As is true in the writing of all books, this has not been strictly a solo work. I have three people, especially, to thank for their behind-the-scenes assistance.

First, my very diligent and determined friend, Judith Markham, whose editorial assistance proved, once again, invaluable.

Second, Mary Hollingsworth, who helped me put the finishing touches on the final manuscript . . . before my deadline!

And third, Julie Meredith, who traced all my quotations, verified their accuracy and secured the permissions in an efficient and timely manner.

My appreciation for these capable ladies knows no bounds. In many ways, you hold this book in your hands because they did their work so well.

Of course, as always, I have my wife, Cynthia, to thank for her encouragement and affirmation. It was our own mysterious (and often *painful)* journey together during recent years that prompted my writing on this subject. Thankfully, she hung in there with me when we had great confusion, few answers, and little strength.

—CHUCK SWINDOLL
Dallas, Texas

Part I

❧

The Buffetings of God's Will

God will not look you over for medals,
degrees, or diplomas, but for scars.

—ELBERT HUBBARD, *The Note Book*

By trying we can easily learn to endure adversity.
Another man's, I mean.

—MARK TWAIN, *Following the Equator*

1

A Process and a Puzzle

The best is perhaps what we understand the least.

—C.S. Lewis, *A Grief Observed*

'Tis very puzzling on the brink of what is called eternity
to stare and know no more of what is *here* than *there*.

—Byron, *Don Juan*

People wish to be settled:
only as far as they are unsettled
is there any hope for them.

—EMERSON, *Essays: First Series*

Chapter One

❦

A Process and a Puzzle

THE FLAG OF SORROW flew at half mast over many an American heart in mid-July, 1999. Another tragedy. Another in a long line of familiar names from the famous Kennedy clan tasted death much earlier than anyone would have predicted . . . and in a way most would never have guessed.

Ironically, this one happened seven short miles off the same shore of the same sleepy resort island where young John played as a lad. Will the sadness never end for this grief-stricken, shock-stunned family? The list is a litany of tragedies and surprises that reads like a modern-day book of lamentations. Horrible assassinations, sudden deaths, carnal scandals, tragic and life-threatening illnesses, and now a desperate search at sea for the remains of three lives that ended as strangely as any of us could have imagined. There are some who have suggested it is some sort of "curse" that haunts them. To be sure, unanswered questions swarm all over the Kennedys.

Regardless of where you and I may stand politically, ethically, and morally—in spite of whether we agree or disagree with their lives and lifestyles—every one of us turns the same three-letter word over and over in our heads: *Why?* We find ourselves wondering how much longer the plague, if that's what it is, will remain and who of their number will be next. It's a mystery.

Even as Christians, who firmly believe in a God of order and compassion, One who "tenderly cares for His own," we cannot deny the reality that much of what He does and most of why He does it falls into that category . . . at least from our vantage point. And it isn't just one family's mystery—we all live with mysteries, not just the rich and famous. They surround all of us through all of life. The healthy and hearty as well as the sick, the handicapped, and the dying. The young and the old. The godly and the godless.

It's time to say it: More often than not we face life in a quandary. Searching, disturbing questions far outnumber absolute, air-tight answers. Even though we love the Lord and are committed to His plan. Even though we obey His Word and seek His will. If we're honest enough to admit it, there are days—no, there are even months—when we simply cannot figure out what God is up to.

The longer I live, the more I believe that one of the most profound subjects in the Christian life is the will of God. The deeper we dig into it, the more we realize how little we know. When we stop and think deeply about the way He leads us along, we must conclude that it is one of the most mysterious subjects in the spiritual life. Yet I've observed that we use words like "It's the will of God" or "We hope God will have His will and way in this" rather glibly.

Someone has said that getting an education is going from an unconscious to a conscious awareness of our own ignorance. When we do a serious study of the will of God, we go from an unconscious to a conscious awareness of how mysteriously He leads us along. Perhaps this explains why our walk with our Lord is often inconsistent and why it is sometimes more of a struggle than a relief. Let's face it: Much of His plan simply doesn't make sense . . . not to us.

So much of understanding this is a matter of the will—not God's will, but our will. I certainly know that in my own heart I do not always really want to do His will.

We say we do, of course. If we were asked to respond with yes or no to the question, all of us would say, "Yes, I want to know His will." But *doing* God's will is another matter entirely, because almost without exception it requires risk and adjustment and change. We don't like that. Even using those words makes us squirm. Experiencing the reality of them is even worse. We love the familiar. We love the comfortable. We love something we can control—something we can get our arms around. Yet the closer we walk with the Lord, the less control we have over our own lives, and the more we must abandon to Him. To give Him our wills and to align our wills to His will requires the abandonment of what we prefer, what we want or what we would choose.

So as we approach this "archaeological study" of the will of God, let's recognize that we dig into it knowing that everything within us will at times resist doing what He wants us to do.

A PUZZLE WE WILL NEVER SOLVE

What is God's will and what is not God's will? How can we know God's will? Is it common to miss God's will or is that even possible? How did God reveal His will in biblical days? Is it the same way He reveals His will today? Are there prerequisites for knowing God's will? Can I really know that I am doing God's will? That I am in His will? If so, how? And if I'm not doing God's will, how do I know that? Can anyone else help me discern God's will? If I do His will does He always reward me?

All these and more are common questions every thoughtful believer grapples with at one time or another in life.

I jokingly say to people at times, "It's easier for me to know God's will for my *wife* than it is for me to know God's will for my *life*." The reality is, of course, that we often operate on that principle. We believe we know what our spouse ought to do, or what our child ought to do, or what our neighbor ought to do, or what our friend ought to do. But the tough thing is knowing what I ought to be doing.

Who can help us discern that? Who can we lean on, rely on? Are there any examples of those who have walked in His will? Or, what about the opposite? Are there any examples of those who have strayed from His will? Is God's will ever a surprise? And if so, why would He choose to surprise us? Is that fair?

In the following pages, I want to grapple with many of these questions in one form or other. But before we begin, I need to make an admission, which will in some ways be a disclaimer. I admit: *This subject is inscrutable.* Please read those four words again. During my years in seminary, one of my mentors used to say, "One of your problems as young theologians is trying to unscrew the inscrutable." So there are times I will say, without reservation or hesitation, "I do not know the answer." It is a profound, unfathomable subject. Although we have been given so much direction and clarification in the Word of God, there is far more that is beyond our human understanding. So determine right now not to let that trouble you—even you perfectionist types who want to sweep every corner clean and get every part of the subject covered and clearly understood. You will never, ever be able to do that with this subject. Benjamin Disraeli put it well: "To be conscious that you are ignorant is a great step to knowledge."

But don't take my word for it. Let's learn from Scripture. Look at Job 9, where Job is answering Bildad, who, along with Eliphaz and Zophar, has come to bring a bit of comfort to his suffering friend, Job. I write that with tongue in cheek, of course, because these guys really came to accuse Job. As Job himself says later on, "Sorry comforters are you all. What a sorry lot of counselors you have been!"

If you take the time to read Job 8, you'll see how Bildad unloads a major guilt trip on Job. Then in 9:1–12 Job responds. You can almost picture him as he throws his arms in the air and cries,

> In truth I know that this is so, but how can a man be in the right before God?
>
> If one wished to dispute with Him [God], he could not answer Him once in a thousand times.
>
> Wise in heart and mighty in strength, who has defied Him without harm?
>
> It is God who removes the mountains, they know not how, when

He overturns them in His anger;
Who shakes the earth out of its place, and its pillars tremble; who commands the sun not to shine, and sets a seal upon the stars;
Who alone stretches out the heavens, and tramples down the waves of the sea;
Who makes the Bear, Orion, and the Pleiades, and the chambers of the south;
Who does great things, unfathomable,
And wondrous works without number.

Job is awed by the Creator who "shakes the earth out of its place." Californians know that feeling well—that uneasy, insecure feeling of the earth shaking beneath them. He speaks of the One who "commands the sun not to shine, and sets a seal on the stars." We can set our watches by these heavenly lights God put in motion from the beginning. He does "great things," says Job, things that are "unfathomable." When it comes to God's workings and plans, we will never be able to say, "Finally, I've got it! I've figured it all out!"—not until we get to heaven, when we will know as we are known.

"The first sound we will hear from every throat when we get to heaven is 'Ahhhh,'" says my good friend Jay Kesler. "Now I see it! Now I realize why. Now it all makes sense before my eyes, this great once-mysterious panorama of events."

My mentor, the late Ray Stedman, had a helpful description of this. I can still remember his talking about moving from earth to heaven: "We move from the very restricted and limited realm to this massive panorama of the whole scene. And it will be good." It all will have worked together for good, including the tragedies and the calamities and the heartaches, the illnesses and diseases and what we call premature deaths, the terrible deformities and birth defects and congenital illnesses. All will unfold, and we will see that God's plan was right. But not until then. That is Job's point:

[He] does great things, unfathomable, and wondrous works without number.

7

Were He to pass by me, I would not see Him; were He to move past me, I would not perceive Him.

Were He to snatch away, who could restrain Him? Who could say to Him, "What art Thou doing?"

(Job 9:10–12)

Who hasn't been tempted to shake a fist at God and cry, "What are You doing?" A child is kidnapped and brutally murdered. "God, what are You doing to us?" A husband drives to the hardware store on Saturday morning and is hit head-on and killed by a drunk driver. Just that quickly he is taken from his wife and family. "What in the world is God up to?" A young mother has routine surgery, develops unforeseen complications, and dies. "God, what are You doing?" It is unfathomable.

So many things that happen in this life are past searching out. I can't explain His plan. I can only unfold from the Scriptures how unfathomable it really is.

The psalmist gives voice to this eloquently in Psalm 139:1–2:

O Lord, Thou hast searched me and known me.
Thou dost know when I sit down and when I rise up;
Thou dost understand my thought from afar.
Thou dost scrutinize my path and my lying down,
And art intimately acquainted with all my ways.

Before I ever have a thought, You know it's on its way. You know when it strikes my brain and what's going to come as a result of it. You know it long before I have the thought. Yet we still have the freedom to think that thought and follow through on that action. This is part of the unfathomable nature of our God. "You know it from afar. You scrutinize my path."

For Christmas one year we bought our children what was called "Ant City." This consisted of clear plastic plates on either side, filled with sand and ants. From our vantage point outside and above, we could see what these busy little creatures were doing underground. We watched as they tunneled their way around, leaving a maze of trails.

In a similar fashion, God scrutinizes our paths. From where we are, tunneling along, all we see is the sand immediately ahead, behind, and beside us. But from His vantage point, He can see exactly where we've been and precisely where we're going. "He is intimately acquainted with all my ways."

I know my wife, Cynthia, very well, but I am not intimately acquainted with *all* her ways, even though we have been married almost forty-five years. As well as I may know my wife or my children or a friend, I will never be "intimately acquainted" with *all* of their ways. My finite nature hinders such knowledge.

God, however, knows each one of us individually. He numbers the very hairs of our head (which is a bigger challenge for some than for others). The hopes, the wayward thoughts, the directions, the decisions, the indecision, the motives, the words we think but don't say . . . He knows all of those.

> Even before there is a word on my tongue,
> Behold O Lord, Thou dost know it all.
> You have enclosed me behind and before,
> You have laid Your hand upon me.
> Such knowledge is too wonderful for me;
> It is too high, I cannot attain to it. (Psalm 139:4–6)

"I may be Your son," David was saying, "and I may write Your music, Lord, and I may be the king of Your people, but, Lord, Your ways are still beyond me. They remain unfathomable to me. I can't understand or explain what You're doing. Such knowledge is too great for me. I can't reach it. I can't attain to it."

Why is it that in the same family one child will go one direction and one another? "It is too high, I cannot attain to it." All of us are sinners. So why does one couple break up in six months and another stay together for sixty years? Why are some individuals called to serve in small, obscure, and difficult places while others serve in comfort in a large arena, surrounded by support. Why, why, why? "It is too high, I cannot attain to it."

So let's settle this point right at the outset. All of these things and so many more we will never understand in this life. Despite all of our searching and all of our study of the Scriptures, we'll never be able to see everything clearly, to fully grasp and understand and answer all the questions. They are beyond our comprehension—a puzzle, a mystery.

In *Keep a Quiet Heart*, Elisabeth Elliott says, "Today is mine. Tomorrow is none of my business. If I peer anxiously into the fog of the future, I will strain my spiritual eyes so that I will not see clearly what is required of me now." [1]

Much of what happens in life we simply have to take by faith. Answers will not be forthcoming. These are the tensions of reality, and if we get marooned on the tensions, we will not be able to travel further. That is as our heavenly Father planned it.

Who can ever explain the events that occurred at Columbine High school in April, 1999, in Littleton, Colorado? The tragedy is beyond our comprehension—fourteen teenagers and one teacher dead, most of them Christians. How could that be? Why would a loving, caring, gracious God—who does all things well—*even permit* such an event? In our minds, none of the above squares with our understanding of goodness and grace. How could it?

Was all that a part of His plan? could it be that, in this strange unfolding of His will, we have failed to leave sufficient room for His permission of evil? Job asked his wife what I now ask you, "Shall we indeed accept good from God and not accept adversity" (Job 2:10)? *It's a mystery* . . . based on how we see things and how we evaluate fairness and how we gauge goodness.

God is the Potter; we are the clay. He's the Shepherd; we are the sheep. He's the Master; we are the servant. No matter how educated we are, no matter how much power and influence we may think we have, no matter how long we have walked with Him, no matter how significant we may imagine ourselves to be in His plans (if any of us could even claim significance), none of that qualifies us to grasp the first particle of why He does what He does when He does it and how He chooses to do it.

> "For My thoughts are not your thoughts,
> Neither are your ways My ways," declares the LORD.
> "For as the heavens are higher than the earth,
> So are My ways higher than your ways,
> And My thoughts than your thoughts."
> (Isaiah 55:8–9)

Oh, the depth of the riches both of the wisdom and knowledge of God! How unsearchable are His judgments and unfathomable His ways! "For who has known the mind of the Lord, or who became His counselor?" (Romans 11:33–34).

In an old work by Origen, *On First Principles,* the great church father underscores what the apostle of grace meant when he wrote that statement:

Paul did not say that God's judgments were hard to search out but that they could not be searched out at all. He did not say that God's ways were hard to find out but that they were impossible to find out. For however far one may advance in the search and make progress through an increasing earnest study, even when aided and enlightened in the mind by God's grace, he will never be able to reach the final goal of his inquiries.[2]

As I think about God's unfathomable ways and the theme of this book, I am reminded of the six-year-old boy who had been given an assignment to draw anything he wanted to draw. But when everyone else in the class had finished drawing, he was still sitting there working on his picture. Finally the teacher walked back and looked over his shoulder.

"What are you drawing?" she asked.

"I'm drawing a picture of God," said the boy.

"You need to remember, Johnny, no one has ever seen God. Nobody knows what He looks like."

"Well . . . they will when I'm through," said Johnny.

That's what I would love to think about this book: that when I have finished writing and the printer has finished printing and all my readers have finished reading, that people will at least know what the will of God looks like. But even though I think we will all have learned some things together, in all humility and reality, I know that you won't find it all, or see it all in these pages. So, don't get your hopes up!

What I hope we will do is learn how to turn to God and rely on Him to work out His will in our lives. Hopefully we will realize the enormity of our own ignorance and our need to trust Him and then let it be. Just let it be. If His plan for you is a surprise or, perhaps, a disappointment, let it be. I urge you to come to terms with the disappointment and accept the surprise. Go ahead . . . call it a mystery. Let Him have His way with your life, for nothing is worse than resisting and resenting the One who is at work in you.

The amazing thing is that even in the midst of disappointment, surprise, and mystery you will discover how very reliable and trustworthy God is—and how secure you are in His hands. And oh, how we need that in this day of relativism and vacillation, filled with empty talk and hidden behind a lot of semantic footwork. In the midst of "spin city," it is the Lord who talks straight. It is the Lord who has preserved Truth in black and white in His Word. And it is the Lord who has the right to do as He wishes around us, to us, and in us. He's the Potter, remember. Puzzling as the process may be to us, He stays with His plan. There is no need for us to know all the reasons, and He certainly doesn't need to explain Himself. Potters work with the clay, they don't fret over it . . . or ask permission to remake the clay into whatever they wish.

And if we're going to let God be God, then we're forced to say He has the right to take us through whatever process He chooses. The journey may be painful as well as puzzling . . . including a tragedy at sea seven miles off Martha's Vineyard and a massacre in a school in Littleton, Colorado.

2

God Decrees . . . God Permits

The way of God is complex, He is hard for us to predict.
He moves the pieces and they come somehow into a
kind of order.

—EURIPIDES, *Helen*

There is something fundamentally flawed about a purely academic interest in God. God is not an appropriate object for cool, critical, detached, scientific observation and evaluation. No, the true knowledge of God will always lead us to worship. . . . Our place is on our faces before Him in adoration.

—JOHN R. W. STOTT, *Romans: God's Great News for the World*

Chapter Two

∞

God Decrees . . . God Permits

THINKING THEOLOGICALLY is a tough thing to do. It works against our human and horizontal perspective on life. Thinking vertically is a discipline few have mastered. We much prefer to live in the here-and-now realm, seeing life as others see it, dealing with realities we can touch, analyze, prove, and explain. We are much more comfortable with the tactile, the familiar, the logic shaped by our culture and lived out in our times.

But God offers a better way to live—one that requires faith, as it lifts us above the drag and grind of our immediate little world, opens new dimensions of thought, and introduces a perspective without human limitations. In order to enter this better way, we must train ourselves to think theologically. Once we've made the switch, our focus turns away from ourselves, removing us from a self-centered realm of existence and opening the door of our minds to a God-centered frame of reference, where all things begin and end with Him.

A prophet named Jeremiah was called by God to minister on His behalf. Jeremiah was afraid to accept the assignment because, from his perspective, he was too young, too inexperienced . . . simply too inadequate. The Lord silenced such horizontal thinking by telling Jeremiah that He knew him even before he was conceived and had set him apart even before he was born. God also promised to protect him and to deliver him and to use him mightily. That started Jeremiah thinking theologically. God had decreed certain things. Jeremiah needed to obey without fear or hesitation. Hard times would surely come—all of which God would permit to happen. But Jeremiah could take great comfort in knowing that God would have His way in spite of the hardships ahead. God had called him and would protect him. And even the opposition Jeremiah would encounter (which God permitted to occur) would not stop or alter God's plan (which He had decreed would occur).

For the rest of this chapter I urge you to think theologically. It will help. By doing so, you will grasp the importance of both the decreed will of God and the permitted will of God.

GOD'S DECRETIVE WILL

The first facet of God's will is what we shall call His decretive will: His sovereign, determined, immutable will. Our friend Job spoke of this when he said,

> Man, who is born of woman,
> Is short-lived and full of turmoil. . . .
> Since his days are determined,
> The number of his months is with Thee,
> And his limits Thou hast set so that he cannot pass.
> (Job 14:1, 5)

Job's words tell us that the decreed will of God is running its course precisely as arranged by our great God. This aspect of the will of God is not something that we can anticipate ahead of time; we can only know it after it has happened.

There are occasions when we are surprised by His decreed will . . . like when we get the results back from our physical exam and the MRI reveals a tumor we had no idea was there. Or when a thirty-seven-year-old wife smiles across the supper table and informs her forty-five-year-old husband, "We're going to have another baby." And their youngest is in high school! Or when the stock market plunges in one day to a ten-year, record-setting low.

It may seem to many that the One who made us is too far removed to concern himself with such tiny details of life on this old globe. But that is not the case. His mysterious plan is running its course right on schedule, exactly as He decreed it.

This world is not out of control, spinning wildly through space. Nor are earth's inhabitants at the mercy of some blind, random fate. When God created the world and set the stars in space, He also established the course of this world and His plan for humanity.

Not all believe this, obviously. To some, this teaching is disturbing and distasteful. And so they go searching for other gods.

Some months ago when I was on a flight to Southern California, my seatmate pulled out a well-worn, thick paperback called *All the Religions of the World.* As he read, I thought to myself, I wish I could take him by the hand and introduce him to the one God who is the Lord of all and over all—the One who satisfies as none of the religions of the world will ever do. I tried, unsuccessfully.

The apostle Paul addressed this very issue when he preached in Athens. The city was filled with idols, for the ancient Athenians had a cast of multiple-thousands when it came to gods and goddesses. They had even erected a monument "To an Unknown God." Then, in a masterful stroke of homiletic genius, Paul said, in effect, "Allow me to introduce you to Him, this God you have missed." (See Acts 17:16–34.)

There is only one God, and He is responsible for the sovereignly decreed plan over this earth.

> I am the LORD, and there is no other;
> Besides Me there is no God.
> I will gird you, though you have not known Me;
> That men may know from the rising to the setting of the sun

> That there is no one besides Me.
> I am the LORD, and there is no other;
> The One forming light and creating darkness,
> Causing well-being and creating calamity;
> I am the LORD who does all these.
> (Isaiah 45:5–7)

Through Isaiah's pen the Lord declares that He is the one who forms light and creates darkness, causes well-being and creates calamity. This is another of those "unexplainables." I don't know why a tornado destroys one neighborhood and not another. I just know that even in this calamity God's plan is not frustrated or altered. Either that, or He isn't God. He is not sitting on the edge of heaven, wondering what will happen next. That's not the God of the Scriptures. So while we cannot fathom the "Why?" of this age-old question, we do know that Scripture states that God is not surprised by calamity. Somehow or other, it's all part of His mysterious will.

Now that is a tough concept to justify. So my advice is quite simple: Quit trying. While this is not the verse you send in a note of comfort to somebody who has just gone through a great tragedy, it is a verse you need to comfort yourself with when you are going through your own calamity. Remember, nothing is a surprise to God, not even our slightest trials. His plan may seem unfair, humanly illogical, and lacking compassion, but that's because we dwell in the here and now. We lack the vertical view. In fact, we sometimes quarrel with God, as the prophet Isaiah testifies:

> "Woe to the one who quarrels with his Maker—
> An earthenware vessel among the vessels of earth!
> Will the clay say to the potter, 'What are you doing?'
> Or the thing you are making say, 'He has no hands'? . . .
> "It is I who made the earth, and created man upon it.
> I stretched out the heavens with My hands,
> And I ordained all their host.

"I have aroused him in righteousness,
And I will make all his ways smooth;
He will build My city, and will let My exiles go free,
Without any payment or reward," says the LORD of hosts.
(Isaiah 45: 9, 12–13)

At one time in my life statements like that made me cringe and become resentful. Not until I released my grip on my horizontal perspective did I find any comfort in God's sovereignty. Little by little, it began to settle in my mind, bringing relief instead of fear. God is in charge, not us! I address this in detail in chapter 5.

This determined, decreed dimension of God's will has four qualities: (1) It is absolute. (2) It is immutable, which means "unchangeable." (3) It is unconditional. (4) It is always in complete harmony with His plan and His nature. In other words, the decreed will of God will be holy, it will be just, it will be good, it will be righteous; therefore, it will be best. And it will all work toward those ends.

The subject of God's will is woven throughout the tapestry of God's truth as revealed in Scripture. We have seen it in Isaiah. Now let's observe it in Romans:

We know that God causes all things to work together for good to those who love God, to those who are called according to His purpose.

For whom He foreknew, He also predestined to become conformed to the image of His Son, that He might be the first-born among many brethren;

and whom He predestined, these He also called; and whom He called, these He justified; and whom He justified, these He also glorified. (Romans 8:28–29)

Mark in the margin of your Bible beside these verses: "Decreed will of God." His decreed will is at work in your life. He's chipping away in your life, causing you to take on the character of His Son, Jesus Christ.

A sculptor was asked how he could carve a lion's head out of a large block of marble. "I just chip away everything that doesn't look like a lion's head," was his reply. God works away in our being and chips away everything that doesn't look like Christ—the impatience, the short temper, the pride, the emotional drives that lead us away from our Father. He's shaping us into His image. That's His predetermined plan. And He's committed to it. Nothing we can do will dissuade Him from that plan. He stays at it. He is relentless. And He never runs out of creative ideas.

That's why He sends one person to the mission field in China and another to the bank building in downtown Seattle. That's part of His sovereign plan to shape individuals into the image of Christ. It doesn't mean that the person who goes to China is holier or more in the will of God than the person who goes into banking. You're wrong only if you don't go where He is leading you. How do you know it was part of His decreed will? Because it has happened. Just glance back over your past. You will be able to identify your own personal list of God's decretive will in your life. Grant Howard in *Knowing God's Will—and Doing It* writes,

> Can I know the determined will of God for my life? Yes—after it has occurred! You now know that God's determined will for your life was that you be born of certain parents, in a certain location, under certain conditions, and that you be male or female. You now know that God determined for you to have certain features, certain experiences, certain teachers, certain interests, certain friends, a certain kind of education, and certain brothers or sisters, or perhaps to be an only child. In other words, everything that has happened in your life to this moment has been part of God's determined will for your life. It has happened because He has determined it to be so.[1]

"Wait a minute, wait a minute," I hear you saying. "I've got a question." We all have questions about this. I told you it was profound. I told you we couldn't understand it. We want to be in charge.

We want to say, "No, this is up to me. I choose my own friends. I choose my own interests. I decided where I wanted to go to college."

Now it's *my* turn to say, "Wait a minute." Who sent out the proclamation that you are now in charge? It's not up to you. You're the clay; He's the Potter. Remember? You're the branch; He's the Vine. You're the servant; He's the Master. It's all in His hands. What a wonderful way to live!

What may seem at the time like a series of mysterious, illogical events is, in fact, God at work in ways too deep to explain, too profound for you to grasp . . . right now. Grant Howard continues,

> What about the future? Can I know any part of God's determined will for my life in the future? Your spiritual position and your eternal destiny are the only two things you can know with certainty. If you are in Christ now, you can know for certain you will remain in Christ at every moment in the future. The remainder of your future is hidden from you until it happens. Your career, your marriage partner, your home location, your grades in school, your sicknesses, accidents, honors, travels, income, retirement are all part of God's determined will but are not revealed ahead of time. Apart from your spiritual position and eternal destiny, all that will happen in your life cannot be predicted with absolute certainty.[2]

Stop and think. Who would have guessed five years ago that you'd be doing what you're doing right now, or that you would have experienced over those five years what you've experienced? Not one of us. And I have news for you. You have no idea what the next five years will bring. The future is just as uncertain and exciting and full of risk and wonder as the past five years you have lived. But whatever that future brings is also absolute, immutable, unconditional, and in complete harmony with God's nature and plan.

"Our God is in the heavens; He does whatever He pleases" (Psalm 115:3). This is the verse Lila Trotman quoted when she heard that her husband, Dawson Trotman, founder of The Navigators, had drowned at Scroon Lake, New York. Dawson plunged into the water to rescue two girls who had been thrown out of a speedboat, and then he himself drowned. The friend who was with him ran down the shoreline and found Lila. "Lila, Dawson's gone," he screamed. "He's gone!" That's when Lila calmly quoted Psalm 115:3. She took comfort in God's determined will. What seemed to many as a premature and untimely death, later was seen as God's perfect plan for the fine organization Daws had founded and launched.

More than once through the years that verse has helped me think theologically, saving me from sleepless nights . . . from hours of agonizing over, *Why?*

Even the death of our Savior was part of the determined will of God:

> Men of Israel, listen to these words: Jesus the Nazarene, a man attested to you by God with miracles and wonders and signs which God performed through Him in your midst, just as you yourselves know—this Man, delivered up *by the predetermined plan and foreknowledge of God,* you nailed to a cross by the hands of godless men and put Him to death. (Acts 2:22–23, italics mine)

Though unbelieving men nailed Jesus to His cross, it occurred, "by the predetermined plan and foreknowledge of God." It was exactly at the time and in the place and by the means God had determined. And what looked to the eleven confused disciples as mysterious, as well as unfair and unjust (humanly speaking, it was all of the above and more), God looked at it and said, "That is what I've planned. That's the mission that My Son came to accomplish."

That's why Jesus' final words from the cross before He died were "It is finished." God's redemption plan had been completed—Jesus' payment for our sin. And then He slumped in death.

> And God raised Him up again, putting an end to the agony of death, since it was impossible for Him to be held in its power. (Acts 2:24)

That's exactly what will happen beyond our death. He will raise us up by His grace, putting an end forever to the agony of death, since we will not be held by its power. God has *decreed* it so. That is a wonderful thought to claim at a graveside, isn't it?

This means, however, that there are some things God cannot and will not do because they do not conform to His nature. For example, God cannot and will not lie (Numbers 23:19; Hebrews 6:18). God cannot and does not tempt anyone to sin (James 1:13–15). Those actions would be against His nature and, therefore, against His will.

"Let no one say when he is tempted, 'I am tempted by God,'" writes James, and he uses an interesting syntax when he writes this. In the original language James used a more subtle expression, meaning, "Let no one say when he is tempted, 'I've been tempted indirectly by God.'"

That's a familiar angle, isn't it? Remember the first couple, Adam and Eve? "The woman You gave me, she caused me to sin." (Indirectly, "Lord, You're the one who made me sin.") And we've been doing that ever since. "Lord, if You hadn't given me this nature, I wouldn't have checked into the Internet, and I wouldn't have gone to that chat room, and I wouldn't have gotten involved with that woman, which led to the affair. I mean, if You hadn't given me the time to do this . . ." Not only is that nonsense, it's terrible theology. God cannot, does not, and will not tempt us. He never solicits us to do evil.

Also, God will never contradict His own nature to make a point. "If we are faithless, He remains faithful; for He cannot deny Himself," Paul writes in 2 Timothy 2:13. God is eternally consistent.

Of course we haven't even scratched the surface of this subject of the decretive will of God, but this at least gives us a place to start.

Just remember: No one ultimately is able to frustrate God's plan . . . no one. No one who lets us down surprises God. No one who walks away from his or her responsibilities causes God to wonder why.

In the final analysis, God will have His way. What He has determined will transpire.

But what about evil? What is God's role regarding earthly matters that do not reflect His holy character?

GOD'S PERMISSIVE WILL

The other realm of the will of God is His permissive will, which represents what God allows. For example, God allowed Job to go through suffering. God didn't cause the suffering. He permitted it.

Satan came to God and accused Job of being one of those individuals whom the Lord had carefully protected. "Who wouldn't trust a God who protects His servant from harm? But you touch Job, you touch his life, you touch his family, you touch his health, and he'll curse You."

"All right," said the Lord. "I will allow you to do all that."

I don't know why God did that. How could He call that fair or merciful? From my perspective, it wasn't. It's part of His mysterious will. But I'm not God. I'm merely the clay; He's the Potter. Admittedly, when we read the whole story, we see what wonderful things Job learned about God through this ordeal.

> Then Job answered the Lord, and said,
> "I know that Thou canst do all things,
> And that no purpose of Thine can be thwarted. . . .
> Therefore I have declared that which I did not understand,
> Things too wonderful for me, which I did not know."
> (Job 42:1–3)

As a result, for succeeding generations, Job's name has been synonymous with patience.

Another example and element of the permissive will of God is found in 2 Peter 3:9:

> The Lord is not slow about His promise, as some count slowness, but is patient toward you, not wishing for any to perish but for all to come to repentance. (2 Peter 3:9)

There's the very top of God's "wish list." He wishes that all would come to Him and repent—that none would perish. But all will not repent; some never will. The apostle Paul said, in effect, "I've done all of these things that I might by all means save some (1 Cor. 9:19–22)." He knew that all would not be saved.

Every time I stand up to preach, I pray, "Lord, bring everyone in this place who is without Christ to Yourself." But I'm a realist. And I know that some will choose not to accept Christ. That's part of His plan. From God's perspective, they are not among the elect. This is a tension—another of those unfathomables, those imponderables. If He's not wishing for any to perish, then why doesn't He save everyone? Because it's not part of His sovereign plan. He predetermined the plan of salvation, knowing that many would refuse it. The plan is set. Fixed. Unchanged and unchanging. But some prefer darkness to light, so they willfully refuse to turn to Christ for salvation.

You see, this is where the whole matter of evil comes into play. And this is one of the irreconcilable difficulties in our theology: the tension between the determined will of God and the responsibility of humanity. We need to make Christ known to the whole world, knowing all the while that not everyone in the world will believe.

Charles Spurgeon, one of the great sovereign grace Baptists of yesteryear, put it well when he said, "If God had put a white stripe down the back of every one of the elect, I'd spend my days in London going up and down the streets lifting up shirttails. But because He said, 'Whosoever will may come,' I preach to them all."

God does not wish for anyone to perish but for all to come to repentance. He does not cause sin, but He does permit it. He is not pleased when His creation yields to temptation, but He uses even that to accomplish His purposes.

Pause right now and read Acts 4:27–31.

"For truly in this city there were gathered together against the holy servant Jesus, whom Thou didst anoint, both Herod and Pontius Pilate, along with the Gentiles and the peoples of Israel, to do whatever Thy hand and Thy purpose predestined to occur.

"And now, Lord, take note of their threats, and grant that Thy bond-servants may speak Thy word with all confidence, while Thou dost extend Thy hand to heal, and signs and wonders take place through the name of Thy holy servant Jesus."

And when they had prayed, the place where they had gathered together was shaken, and they were all filled with the Holy Spirit, and began to speak the word of God with boldness.

You will find the disciples preaching out in the open, telling both Jews and Gentiles about the death and resurrection of Jesus. They are dodging verbal bullets right and left. Then they retreat a bit and regroup, encourage each other, and go back out to witness to God's offer of salvation to all people. They are scourged and whipped and threatened, only to return again . . . they're back out preaching. They are tortured and imprisoned, and they're still witnessing. It reminds me of one of those big plastic punching dolls: you keep knocking it down and it keeps bouncing right back up. This is one of those bouncing-back-up moments.

In His permissive will, God used godless Gentiles like Pontius Pilate and Herod to carry out His purposes and plans. No matter what our station or status in life, we're all servants—one way or the other—of the sovereign Lord of the universe. He can do whatever He wills with any of us.

DO WE KNOW ANYTHING FOR SURE?

God's Word clearly declares that certain things are not the will of God and never will be the will of God in the Christian life. It also clearly teaches that certain things are the will of God for the believer. We don't have to pray to "find leading" on this. We only have to dig through the Scriptures to mine it for ourselves. Once unearthed, these truths sparkle like the richest ore or brightest gemstone.

This is solid, immutable, unchangeable, biblical, God-given truth. The unsaved will never understand it, nor should we try to make them live up to it. This is strictly the will of God for the child of God. For example, sexual immorality is never the will of God.

> For this is the will of God, your sanctification; that is, that you abstain from sexual immorality. (1 Thessalonians 4:3)

I'm reminded of the Ten Commandments here—a full and complete list of divine prohibitions (read Exodus 20:3–17). Another clearly stated set of actions God hates is conveyed in Proverbs 6:16–19.

Now that we've looked at a few of the negatives, let's consider some of the things that Scripture explicitly tells us are the will of God for our lives.

> Rejoice always; pray without ceasing; in everything give thanks; for this is God's will for you in Christ Jesus. (1 Thessalonians 5:16–18)

"Should I give thanks? Is that the will of God for my life?" You don't have to pray about that. He says it here loud and clear: Rejoice. Pray without ceasing. Give thanks in everything. Give thanks when you are being tested, stretched, and forced to wait. Yes, give thanks. Give thanks for the patience you are learning. Give thanks for the way God is working in your life through this trial. Give thanks.

Peter, one of Jesus' closest friends, reminds us of two more responses that are always the will of God. The first has to do with submission. The second relates to an obedient walk in a wayward world.

> Submit yourselves for the Lord's sake to every human institution, whether to a king as the one in authority, or to governors as sent by him for the punishment of evildoers and the praise of those who do right.
>
> For such is the will of God that by doing right you may silence the ignorance of foolish men. (1 Peter 2:13–15)

While we may not know what the will of God is for the future, He has given us a whole list of requirements that are in His will for every believer:

- Obey your parents (Ephesians 6:1)
- Marry a Christian (1 Corinthians 6:15)
- Work at an occupation (1 Thessalonians 4:11–12)
- Support your family (1 Timothy 5:8)
- Give to the Lord's work and to the poor (2 Corinthians 8—9; Galatians 2:10)
- Rear your children by God's standards (Ephesians 6:4)
- Meditate on the Scriptures (Psalm 1:2)
- Pray (1 Thessalonians 5:17)
- Have a joyful attitude (1 Thessalonians 5:16)
- Assemble for worship (Hebrews 10:25)
- Proclaim Christ (Acts 1:8)
- Set proper values (Colossians 3:2)
- Have a spirit of gratitude (Philippians 4:6)
- Display love (1 Corinthians 13)
- Accept people without prejudice (James 2:1–10)

And the list goes on and on.

This is the will of God for your life as a child of God, no matter who you are or where you live. Nothing mysterious here!

The better you get to know the Word of God, the less confusing is the will of God. Those who struggle the least with the will of God are those who know the Word of God best.

We see the importance of the Scriptures clearly when we consider another of those often-asked questions: How did God reveal His will in biblical times? And does He do the same today?

LOOKING FOR GUIDANCE

"God's guidance in the Old Testament reached down into the details of daily life while His guidance in the New Testament is expressed in more general commands and principles," says Garry Friesen in his book *Decision Making and the Will of God.*[3]

In biblical times, God revealed His will in a number of ways, but most of them fall into three categories that are clearly verified in Scripture.

First, God used miraculous events to reveal His will.

Before there was Genesis through Revelation, before there was a completed, written revelation of the mind of God, He occasionally used miracles to reveal His will. Examples? The burning bush (Exodus 3:1–10). How did Moses know it was God telling him to return to Egypt and deliver the Israelites? The burning bush. The fact that a bush burned in the wilderness wasn't a miracle. That happens to this day. Lightning strikes, and poof, foliage catches fire and burns. But this brush fire wouldn't go out. Miraculously, it burned and burned. And that's what caused Moses to stop and listen and hear God's will.

Or what about the Red Sea? How did Moses know he should cross the Red Sea? The sea miraculously opened up, making a dry pathway for Moses and the Israelites (Exodus 14:21–29). Pretty sure indication that it was God's will for him to walk across, right?

In the time of the Judges, Gideon wanted to know God's will. He left a lamb fleece out overnight, and God indicated His will by leaving dew on the fleece one time, and another time, no dew (Judges 6).

In the days of the early church, how did Peter know that it was God's will for him to leave prison? God opened the doors and brought him out miraculously (Acts 12:1–16).

Today, God rarely reveals His will through miraculous events. People may think they see a miracle—like a parking place at the mall during Christmas season or the face of Jesus in an enchilada—but that's not the way God works today. As my friend Gary Richmond says, "If miracles happened that often, they'd be called regulars."

Not that God no longer does miracles. He does. But miracles, by their very definition, are extremely rare. In my lifetime, I probably could name three I've been aware of, and they were so obviously miracles of God that no other explanation would work. But God's standard method of revealing His will is not through miracles. So, please, don't get caught in that trap. Guard against anticipating or searching for miracles to find God's will. You don't need them.

God used miracles in ancient times because that was the way He spoke to His people prior to His Word being written. Today, He speaks to us through His Word.

Second, God spoke through visions and dreams.

Abraham saw visions, and Joseph dreamed dreams (Genesis 15:1; 40:8; 41:25). God spoke to Abraham through visions, just as He spoke to Joseph through dreams. He even used an Egyptian Pharaoh's dreams and Joseph's interpretation of those dreams to preserve Egypt from the ravages of a terrible drought and famine. God worked His will for both the Israelites and the Egyptians through visions and dreams.

In New Testament times, Peter saw a sheet coming down from heaven with all kinds of food on it—including what would have been the equivalent of a ham sandwich to a Jew. He saw food that God had forbidden the Jews to eat. Now, however, God said, "Eat." Peter said, "I can't eat." And God said, "Eat." Through this vision of the sheet and the miraculous provision of this food, Peter discovered that it was God's will for him to take the gospel message to the Gentiles (Acts 10:10–23).

Third, God revealed His will through direct revelation.

God spoke His will to His prophets, who in turn delivered the message to the people. "Amos, do this." "Isaiah, say that." "Jeremiah, go over there." The prophets spoke as oracles of God. "For no prophecy was ever made by an act of human will, but men, moved by the Holy Spirit spoke from God" (2 Peter 1:21).

The Greek word here is *pherō,* and it literally means to be "moved along apart from one's own power." It's a nautical term used for a ship without a rudder or a sail, carried along at the mercy of the waves and the wind and the current. Here the word is used for the prophets, moved not by their own power, but by the power of God as He spoke through them and revealed His will.

God no longer speaks through prophets. I don't care what they tell you on television. Or, to quote John Stott:

The Christian preacher is not a prophet. That is, he does not derive his message from God as a direct and original revelation. Of course, the word "prophet" is used loosely by some people today. It is not uncommon to hear a man who preaches with passion described as possessing prophetic fire; and a preacher who can discern the signs of the times, who sees the hand of God in the history of the day and seeks to interpret the significance of political and social trends, is sometimes said to be a prophet and to have prophetic insight. But I suggest this kind of use of the title "prophet" is an improper one.[4]

What, then, is a prophet? The Old Testament regarded him as the immediate mouthpiece of God. . . . the prophet was God's "mouth," through whom God spoke His words to man. The prophet spoke neither his own words nor in his own name. . . . The Christian preacher, therefore, is not a prophet. No original revelation is given to him; his task is to expound the revelation which has been given once for all. (Jude 3). The last occurrence in the Bible of the formula "the word of God came unto" refers to John the Baptist (Luke 3:2). He was a true prophet.

Now that the written word of God is available to us all, the word of God in prophetic utterance is no longer needed. The word of God does not come to men today. It has come once and for all; men must now come to it.

Gaining a clear understanding of this concept will save you days of heartache and months of confusion. How many times have you heard someone say, "The Lord told me to do so and so"? I confess to you, in my unguarded moments I want to ask, "Was His voice a baritone or a bass? You're telling me you heard His voice?" Of course when people say they have actually heard God's voice, I get even more spooked!

Have you exhausted His Word so completely that you now must

have a literal voice to guide you? Never! We have an inexhaustible source of truth in God's Word. Go there. It will never contradict God's plan or work against God's nature. You can rely on it. It has come down to us through the centuries. As we derive precepts and principles from the Scriptures, based on a careful, intelligent interpretation of His truth, we're able to apply it in numerous ways to our circumstances today. God's Word and God's will are inseparably connected. His Word is God's final revelation, until He sends His Son and takes us home to be with Him. Yes . . . *final*.

> God, after He spoke long ago to the fathers in the prophets in many portions and in many ways, in these last days has spoken to us in His Son, whom He appointed heir of all things, through whom also He made the world. (Hebrews 1:1–2)

Tell me you have determined God's will from the Scriptures, carefully studied within the context in which it was given, and you've got my attention and my respect. Don't regale me with tales of a night vision or some "word of knowledge" in a dream. Don't talk to me about a voice, especially one you heard in the middle of the night while standing in your kitchen. (It was probably just a bad case of indigestion.) I don't mean to be flippant about serious spiritual matters, but this kind of extra-biblical revelation is not only spurious, it's downright dangerous. It invariably leads you astray, away from the truth of God. Your curiosity and your fascination will take over, eclipsing the authority of the Scriptures.

Those who have a high view of biblical revelation, I find, have a very low view of any kind of extra-biblical revelation. Can God do it? Certainly. He is God, and He is able to do whatever He pleases. Does God do it? In all my years of ministry, I've never found a reliable incident of such revelation. On the other hand, I've seen sincere people get into a lot of trouble and confusion because they relied on extra-biblical truth rather than on the Word of God.

Several years ago I witnessed this in the lives of a fine pastor and his wife. Originally in his ministry, this gifted young man was committed to the clear and practical exposition of the Word. The church he was pastoring grew, not only in numbers but also in harmony as they related to one another in love. It was a strong, healthy body.

Then, through an intriguing chain of events, the pastor and his wife began to rely more on dreams and visions for direction and less on the truth of the Scriptures. The congregation became divided as some in the flock began to seek God's will through various extrabiblical phenomena while others resisted such teaching. Ultimately, the rift fractured the fellowship. The pastor left and began another church a few miles away as his loyal followers joined him, while others stayed to pick up the pieces. Hard feelings and broken relationships now remain. Confusion has replaced harmony. The final authority of that pastor is no longer based on the written Word of God but, more and more, on dreams, visions, strange interpretations of the Bible, and erroneous teaching that highlights experience.

God's Word provides all the light we will ever need on our journey through this life. It's "a lamp to our feet and a light to our path (Psalms 119:105)." It brings light to our darkened minds. It helps us think theologically. Strange and mysterious though His leading may seem, when we derive our understanding from a serious investigation of the written Word of God, we will not be led astray. And we will continue to stand on the solid rock of God's Word of truth.

All other ground is sinking sand.

3

Moving from Theory to Reality

Moving from failure to failure
without any loss of enthusiasm.

—WINSTON CHURCHILL'S DEFINITION OF SUCCESS

Confusion is a word we have invented
for an order which is not understood.

—HENRY MILLER, *Tropic of Capricorn*

Chapter Three

❧

Moving From Theory to Reality

I'M TOTALLY CONFUSED . . . How in the world do I find the will of God for my life?" I cannot number how many times through the years I have heard that question. It's a dilemma that has caused people to devise some very strange methods to reach some even stranger conclusions.

Years ago, I read about a man who was driving through Washington, D.C., when his car stalled in front of the Philippine Embassy. He took that to mean that he should be a missionary to the Philippines.

Then there was the woman who wasn't sure she ought to go on a trip to Israel. One night she was reading through the travel brochures and tour information and noticed that the flight was to be on a 747. She woke up the next morning, saw 7:47 on her digital clock, and took that as a sign she should go to Israel.

This sort of nonsense is what I call "voodoo theology." It is nothing more than superstition. We must guard ourselves from being lured into this kind of thinking.

God has spelled out many of His directives very clearly in Scripture, as we saw in the previous chapter, but many of the things we grapple with are not specifically dealt with in His Word. I'll give you some examples.

You've got a son who excels in a particular sport and several fine universities have offered him scholarships. Which school do you choose? Well, that can be a tough choice, but you'll never find the specific answer in a verse of Scripture. If you do, you're reading something into it.

You're single and dating, praying for God to lead you to the right mate for life. But there's nothing in the Bible that states, "Marry John" or "Don't marry Shirley" or "You should date Frank." God gives general principles in His Word—for example, "Do not be unequally yoked together with unbelievers"—but we have to apply them.

You have a good job in Southern California, but you're tired of the smog and the traffic-clogged commute. A company in Colorado offers you a similar position at the same income level. Should you move or stay where you are? A number of factors will enter into your decision, but you will not find the answer directly stated in the Scriptures. If you think you do, you're getting weird.

We sincerely want these specific decisions in our lives to be in accordance with God's will. Deep within, we wish His specific directives would be spelled out in the Scriptures. We'd love to have Him lead us by the hand . . . how reassuring that would be! One of our great old hymns puts it this way: "Guide me, O Thou great Jehovah, / Pilgrim through this barren land; / I am weak, but Thou art mighty; / Hold me with Thy powerful hand." Wouldn't it be a relief to take God by His powerful hand and let Him lead you where He wants you to go?

We don't want to miss God's best for our lives. We want to be held on a steady course by His guiding presence. So, where do we find that guidance, that leading? Let's start by looking at some of the essential prerequisites that help us determine God's will. Thankfully, these are neither ambiguous nor mysterious.

PREREQUISITES FOR FOLLOWING THE WILL OF GOD

First and foremost, you must be a Christian. "For all who are being led by the Spirit of God, these are sons of God" (Romans 8:14).

When you accept Christ as the Savior and Lord of your life, the Holy Spirit comes to dwell within you. Among other things, He is there to reveal the will of God to you. Only the believer has the Spirit's presence within, and we must have this inside help if we are going to follow the will of God.

Second, you must be wise. "Therefore be careful how you walk, not as unwise men, but as wise, making the most of your time, because the days are evil" (Ephesians 5:15–16).

At the beginning of the chapter, I gave you a couple of examples of the foolishness that can occur when people attempt to decipher God's will in the wrong way. God tells us not to be foolish, but wise, making the most of our time, taking every opportunity that comes our way and using it wisely.

Before his twentieth birthday, Jonathan Edwards, the brilliant and godly philosopher-theologian who became God's instrument in the Great Awakening revival of the eighteenth century, resolved "Never to lose one moment of time, but to improve it in the most profitable way I possibly can." That is exactly what he did, using well the intellectual gifts God had given him. He entered Yale at thirteen and at seventeen graduated at the head of his class. At twenty-six he was the minister of one of the largest congregations in Massachusetts.

Scripture says that doing the will of the Lord requires wisdom, for, as Paul writes in the next verse, those who are wise, those who are not foolish, "understand what the will of the Lord is."

Following the will of God requires wisdom, clear thinking, and, yes, even good old garden-variety common sense. Such a mixture helps us understand the Father's will.

Third, you must really want to do the will of God. "If any man is willing to do His will, he shall know of the teaching, whether it is of God, or whether I speak from Myself" (John 7:17).

Your "want to" is a green light: You really will do what He wants you to do. You really want to do the will of God more than anything else. More than completing your education, more than getting married, more than getting your house paid for; more than anything else you want to do the will of God.

Looking back on my own life, I know that there have been times when I said I wanted to do His will but I really didn't. That's a tough thing to confess, but looking back with 20/20 hindsight, I realize that at times I resisted His will. I've learned that serious consequences follow selfish resistance.

The apostle Paul offers words of counsel to those who were enslaved. They have great meaning for us in this context. "Slaves, be obedient to those who are your masters according to the flesh, with fear and trembling, in the sincerity of your heart, as to Christ," wrote Paul, "not by way of eyeservice, as men-pleasers, but as slaves of Christ, doing the will of God *from the heart*" (Ephesians 6:5–6, emphasis added).

Doing the will of God from the heart—that's as deep as it gets. More than pleasing people, more than staying comfortable and safe, you want to please God. You want to follow His will with all of your being.

Fourth, you must be willing to pray and to wait. "Ask, and it shall be given to you; seek, and you shall find; knock, and it shall be opened to you. For everyone who asks receives, and he who seeks finds, and to him who knocks it shall be opened" (Matthew 7:7–8). "And this is the confidence which we have before Him, that, if we ask anything according to His will, He hears us. And if we know that He hears us in whatever we ask, we know that we have the requests which we have asked from Him" (1 John 5:14–15).

Knowing and then following the will of God at times can be a lengthy and painful process. Back in the early 1990s both the president and the chairman of the board of Dallas Seminary asked me to consider becoming the next president of that school. For more than twenty years I had been the pastor of a church in Fullerton,

California. I was not looking for a change, nor did I feel any urgent "push" to entertain their offer. In fact, I spent only a small amount of time in prayer and discussion with my wife before I wrote a letter to the president and the chairman, stating that I had no sense of God's leading me in that direction. As I recall, I listed several "airtight" reasons I should not make such a change in my career. All of these reasons made good sense, which led me to believe I should not consider the issue any further. I wrote a convincing two-page letter that made perfect logical sense . . . but it was wrong!

The Spirit of God would not leave me alone. In subtle yet definite ways He kept bringing the thought back to my mind. I'd shove it aside, only to have Him bring it back. I would ignore the prompting within, but He would not allow me to go very long without another thought returning, prodding me to reconsider. A painful struggle followed. The mystery mushroomed in my mind.

In the meantime, several other events transpired, forcing me to return to the subject. God was going to have His way, whether I was open or not! He refused to leave me alone. There were other phone calls, visits, protracted times spent in prayer and with the Scriptures, conversations with those I respected, and restless nights. Finally, my heart was turned in that direction and I found myself unable to resist any longer. By the end of 1993, I had come full circle: it was the Father's will. I could deny it no longer. Surprised and amazed, I said yes.

Fifth, following the will of God means you must be willing to give up your creature comforts. "And now, behold, bound in spirit, I am on my way to Jerusalem, not knowing what will happen to me there, except that the Holy Spirit solemnly testifies to me in every city, saying that bonds and afflictions await me. But I do not consider my life of any account as dear to myself, in order that I may finish my course, and the ministry which I received from the Lord Jesus, to testify solemnly of the gospel of the grace of God" (Acts 20:22–24).

Here, Paul speaks of the direction in which the Spirit is leading him as being "bound in the spirit." He is caught up in following the will of God, committed to it, bound by it. "I'm leaving you folks here in Ephesus," he says, "and I'm going where it's not going to be as comfortable. In fact, there will be struggles, pressures, discomforts, and afflictions—dangerous risks, even imprisonment. But none of that matters. Even my life doesn't matter."

We're in a process; we're on a journey. If we are to finish the course well, according to the will of our Lord, we must be willing to face some tough things on the journey. Among them will be the loss of things familiar and the need to make some major adjustments.

Now we know some of the essentials that are required before we can even think of following the Lord's will. Yet even if all those are in place, or at least we are committed to them, where do we go next? If we are going to follow, we have to be able to sense the presence and pleasure of our Leader. So, then, how does God lead us into His will today? Without removing all the mystery that often accompanies His will, I have found several absolutes that assist me in following the Lord.

HOW DOES GOD LEAD TODAY?

I could probably list at least ten ways that God leads His children today, but I will limit myself to the four that I think are the most significant methods of God's leading.

First and most basic, God leads us through His written Word. As the psalmist said, "Thy word is a lamp to my feet, and a light to my path" (Psalm 119:105).

Whenever you see the scriptural phrase "This is the will of God," you know for sure that's His will. You also know that to disobey is to break His Word. Other clear indications of His leading are the precepts and principles in the Scripture.

Precepts are clearly marked statements like "Abstain from sexual immorality." That's like saying, "Speed Limit 35." What is speeding? Anything over thirty-five miles an hour. That's a precept.

Then there are principles in the Scriptures, and these are general guidelines that require discernment and maturity if we are to grasp them. Paul writes of "the peace of God" guarding and guiding our hearts and our minds (Philippians 4:7). That's like the sign that says, "Drive Carefully." This may mean forty miles an hour on a clear, uncongested highway, or it may mean ten miles an hour on an ice-covered curve. But it always means that we must be alert and aware of conditions; it always means we have to be discerning. There is no sign large enough to list all the options you have when you're behind the wheel. So you must know the rules of the road, follow the signs that are there, and use all your skill combined with discernment.

There are precepts in Scripture, but mainly God has given us principles to follow. These principles require wisdom and discernment. "Teach me good discernment and knowledge," wrote the psalmist, "for I believe in Thy commandments" (Psalm 119:66).

So often in the emotion of the moment or the pressure of the day, we make a decision that we would never make in the clear, discerning light of God's Word. I recall a couple that came to me for marital counseling several years ago. Their marriage wasn't working, and they had come to the hurried conclusion that what they needed to pull them together was a dog, or maybe a baby. God bless 'em, if the marriage was in trouble, a baby certainly wouldn't fix it, and neither would a dog. Maybe the problem was that one was a believer and the other was not. Perhaps one was not honoring the other. Whatever was needed, I assured them that the principles to follow can be found in the Bible.

You will never, ever go wrong in consulting the Scriptures. Just be sure you take it in context. First Corinthians 7, for example, is all about marriage and remarriage and the struggles in marriage. It's a crucial chapter with very practical advice, but you have to examine all of those verses in their context. Don't use the "open-window method," letting the wind blow across the pages of your Bible and then closing your eyes and pointing to a verse and saying, "This is God's leading on this." If you do that, you could end up with "Judas went away and hanged himself" as your verse for the day! Don't go there.

Would you want to go to a doctor with an ailment and have him say, without ever examining you, "It's your gallbladder?" You ask, "How do you know?" And he'd say, "Well, I sat by the window a few minutes ago and trusted God to blow the pages of my anatomy book to the problem—and the subject on the page was gallbladder." You'd get out of there pretty quick, wouldn't you?

But there are people who make their decisions in life this way— on Philippine Embassies and 747s, on the mood of the moment. And many of them are so sincere that my heart goes out to them. They practice this kind of theological voodoo and then they get in a mess and they say, "Well, God led me" when God had nothing whatsoever to do with their decisions.

So we need to be very clear about the way God leads His people today. God leads us through His written Word. However, keep in mind that this does not mean that we must have a particular Bible verse for every single decision or move we make.

Second, God leads us through the inner prompting of the Holy Spirit. Read the following statement carefully: "So then, my beloved, just as you have always obeyed, not as in my presence only, but now much more in my absence, work out your salvation with fear and trembling; for it is God who is at work in you, both to will and to work for His good pleasure" (Philippians 2:12–13).

Now that you've been born again, Paul says, work out your salvation. In other words, be discerning, think it through, use your head, pay attention, get serious about your Christian walk. For it is God (the Holy Spirit) who is working His will in you. That's why the apostle can say in the next verse, "Do all things without grumbling or disputing" (Philippians 2:14). As the Spirit of God within you engages in various ways of leading you, working out God's will in you, you come to accept it, regardless of the challenges the future brings.

God leads you to a hot, desert-like setting, and you go without grumbling and disputing. You have been married for six months and your spouse is stricken with a debilitating disease that puts her in a wheelchair. You face it "without grumbling and disputing." Though you don't understand how, you trust that it's part of the plan. I could tell you at least half a dozen stories of people who have lived through this kind of trial and come through with magnificent testimonies. One of the most universally recognizable, of course, is Joni Eareckson Tada, whose testimony has touched the lives of multiple-thousands of people. I also think of a young Christian couple who for the past fifteen years have been living through unbelievably difficult circumstances. When they were in their late twenties, parents of four children, the young mother was diagnosed with multiple sclerosis. Now in their thirties, with her condition worsening severely, they are still living witnesses of God's grace "without grumbling and disputing." That is clearly the result of the Holy Spirit's work within.

The inner prompting of the Holy Spirit gives us a sense of God's leading, although that leading is not always what we might call a "feel-good" experience. In my own life, as I mentioned earlier, my decision to accept the presidency of Dallas Seminary was not an easy one. Ultimately, it was an at-peace decision, but it was not what I would have wanted or chosen. Remember my story? I found all kinds of ways to resist when the position was first offered to me. Remember that two-page, airtight letter, carefully thought through, full of Scripture? It should have convinced anybody that I was the wrong person for the job. Except that God was busy convincing them—and, later, me—that I *was* the right person. Although it went against my own wishes at the time, I could not resist the sovereign, all-powerful prompting of the Holy Spirit.

The Book of Jude offers a wonderful example of this: "Beloved, while I was making every effort to write you about our common salvation, I felt the necessity to write to you appealing that you contend earnestly for the faith which was once for all delivered to the saints" (Jude 3). Jude started to write a letter to his fellow Christians about salvation, about the finished work of Christ on the cross. That was his original plan . . . until the Holy Spirit prompted him to do otherwise. "I felt the necessity to do so," Jude admits. I've underlined that phrase in my Bible: "I felt the necessity." That was nothing less than the inner prompting from the Spirit of God.

In similar fashion, I felt the necessity of reconsidering the invitation to Dallas Seminary. So I can testify from personal experience that you can believe you really know God's will, and you may be dead wrong. But if you are, the prompting of the Holy Spirit will be nudging you within. "The mind of man plans his way, but the LORD directs his steps" (Proverbs 16:9).

Nothing wrong with planning. Nothing wrong with thinking it through. Nothing wrong with doing your charts, listing all the pros and cons, talking it over. But as you are moving along, stay sensitive to the quiet, yet all-important prompting of God through His Holy Spirit. It's easier to steer a moving car. Just get the car rolling and you can push it into the filling station to get the gas. But it's hard to get it moving from a dead stop. So you're on your way, you're making your plans, you're thinking it through. Just stay open. By doing so, you may well sense inner promptings that will spur a thought such as, "I can't believe I'm still interested in that. I wonder what the Lord's doing? I wonder where He's going with this?"

As author Henry Blackaby says, "Watch to see where God is at work and join Him!" Just go there. Why do you want to be anywhere God isn't at work?[1]

"I will instruct you and teach you in the way which you should go," says the Lord. "I will counsel you with My eye upon you" (Psalm 32:8). The Spirit of God inside is steering us.

That inner prompting is crucial, because much of the time we just can't figure it out. "Man's steps are ordained by the LORD, how then can man understand his way" (Proverbs 20:24)? (I love that!) When all is said and done, you'll say, "Honestly, I didn't figure this thing out. It must have been God." Talk about mysterious! The longer I live the Christian life, the less I know about why He leads as He does. But I do know that He leads.

The third way God leads us is through the counsel of wise, qualified, trustworthy people. This does not mean some guru in Tibet or serious-looking stranger at the bus stop. This is an individual who has proven himself or herself wise and trustworthy and, therefore, qualified to counsel on a given matter. Usually such individuals are older and more mature than we. Furthermore, they have nothing to gain or lose. This also means that they are often not in our immediate family. (Immediate family members usually don't want us to do something that will take us away from them, or cause us or them discomfort or worry.)

One well-known exception to this is Moses, who listened to the wise counsel of his father-in-law, Jethro (Exodus 18:19–27). "Moses, you're trying to take on too much," said Jethro. "You can't do everything. You need help." Moses listened, and he found that the will of God was that he delegate most of his numerous responsibilities.

At critical moments in my own life, I have sought the counsel of seasoned individuals—and they've seldom been wrong. That's been my experience. But you must choose your counselors very carefully. And just as the best counselors are often not your family, often they are not your best friends either. Wise and trustworthy counselors are persons who want for you only what God wants. Such persons will stay objective, listen carefully, and answer slowly. Often they won't give you an answer at the time you ask for it. They want to sleep on it; they want to think about it.

Finally, God leads us into His will by giving us an inner assurance of peace. "And let the peace of Christ rule in your hearts," Paul writes to the Colossians, "to which indeed you were called in one body; and be thankful" (Colossians 3:15). God's inner assurance of peace will act as an umpire in your heart.

Although peace is an emotion, I have found it wonderfully reassuring as I've wrestled with the Lord's will. This God-given peace comes in spite of the obstacles or the odds, regardless of the risk or danger. It's almost like God's way of saying, "I'm in this decision . . . trust Me through it."

The will of God for our lives is not some high-sounding theory; it is reality. We have discussed some of the prerequisites and requirements for following the will of God, and we have looked at some of the ways God leads us into His will. Now comes the bottom line: We have to live out His will in the real world. In his fine book *Experiencing God*, Henry Blackaby gives some good advice about doing exactly that.

First, doing God's will leads to what he calls a "crisis of belief." That "is a turning point or a fork in the road that demands you make a decision." Doing God's will demands a decision. And that decision requires *faith* and *action*. You can't see the end, so you have to trust Him in faith and then step out. You have to act. Faith and action are like twins; they go together.[2]

Imagine how hard it must have been for Moses to take that first step into the Red Sea. But his faith required action. Before he could get across, he had to take that first step. And as he did, God opened up a dry path through the sea. Blackaby writes,

> God is wanting to reveal Himself to a watching world. He does not call you to get involved just so people can see what you can do. He calls you to an assignment that you cannot do without Him. The assignment will have God-sized dimensions. . . . Some people say, "God will never ask me to do something I can't do." I have come to the place in my life that, if the assignment I sense God is giving me is something I know I can handle, I know it probably is *not* from God. The kind of assignments God gives in the Bible are always God-sized. They are always beyond what people can do because He wants to demonstrate His nature, His strength, His provision, His kindness to His people and to a watching world. That is the only way the world will come to know Him.[3]

Hebrews 11:6 tells us that "without faith it is impossible to please Him, for he who comes to God must believe that He is, and that He is a rewarder of those who seek Him." Following God's will means that we must believe that God is who He says He is and that He will do what He says He will do.

When Cynthia and I started Insight for Living back in 1979, we were total novices. We had no background in radio, no understanding of the world of media, and virtually no money to buy air time. Neither of us even listened to Christian radio. But that was where the Lord's God-sized plan took us. For two uninterrupted decades, we have had to believe that God is who He says He is and will do what He says He will do. We'll be backed into a corner, with seemingly no way out, so we just have to trust Him. And He will move in a special way to give us direction. When it comes time to roll the credits, His name is the name that should be there.

God-sized assignments not only require trust, they also require major adjustments. I have never seen an exception to this rule: *Major adjustments accompany God's will.* Moving from theory to reality in the will of God means risk and release, which spell change. To quote from Blackaby once again:

Good message

You cannot continue life as usual or stay where you are, and go with God at the same time. That is true throughout Scripture. Noah could not continue life as usual and build an ark at the same time. Abram could not stay in Ur or Haran and father a nation in Canaan. Moses could not stay on the back side of the desert herding sheep and stand before Pharaoh at the same time. David had to leave his sheep to become the king. Amos had to leave the sycamore trees in order to preach in Israel. Jonah had to leave his home and overcome a major prejudice in order to preach in Nineveh. Peter, Andrew, James, and John had to leave their fishing businesses to follow Jesus. Matthew had to leave his tax collector's booth to follow Jesus. Saul (later Paul) had to completely change directions in life in order to be used of God to preach the gospel to the Gentiles.[4]

TWO SEARCHING QUESTIONS

Let me ask you two pointed questions as we wrap up our thoughts in this chapter. First: *What makes risk so difficult for you?* Be painfully honest as you answer that question. Blow away the fog in your thinking. Clear out the nettles and overgrown vines of tradition or bad habits or just plain sloth. Change, for most folks, is enormously challenging. Walking with the Lord is a risky path, and everything within us, when we live and lean on our own understanding, screams, "Just keep it like it is. Just leave it alone. If it ain't broke, don't fix it." But sometimes things need to be rearranged even though they aren't broken. Sometimes we need a major change of direction—not because we are necessarily going in an evil direction, it's just not the direction God wants for us. God does not want us to substitute the good for the very best.

Now, here's my second question: *Are you willing to make a major change in your life—assuming that it's the Lord's will?* I'm now convinced that the real issue is not so much "What does the Lord want me to do?" as it is, "Am I willing to do it, once He makes it clear?"

Before moving on into the next chapter, stop and answer those two questions. Not until they are answered are you ready to move ahead, fleshing out the will of God.

4

Fleshing Out the Will of God

The years that lie behind you, with all their struggles and pains, will in time be remembered only as the way that led to your new life. Bur as long as the new life is not fully yours, your memories will continue to cause you pain. When you keep reliving painful events of the past, you can feel victimized by them.

—HENRI NOUWEN, *The Inner Voice of Love*

A holy life isn't the automatic consequence of reading the right books, listening to the right tapes, or attending the right meetings. It's the result of a living, loving union with Jesus Christ and a life marked by godly discipline..

—WARREN WIERSBE, *On Being a Servant of God*

Chapter Four

∽

Fleshing Out the Will of God

So much for general information. Now it's time for personal involvement. The truth is, our problem is not a lack of knowledge but an absence of passion . . . a reluctance to do what we believe God would have us do. I've met some who excuse their lack of involvement by claiming that God does it all. After all, He is sovereign. He, alone, makes things happen.

In his book *The Knowledge of the Holy,* A. W. Tozer gives this simple but helpful illustration of the will and sovereignty of God.

If in His absolute freedom God has willed to give man limited freedom, who is there to stay His hand or say, "What doest thou?" Man's will is free because God is sovereign. A God less than sovereign could not bestow moral freedom upon His creatures. He would be afraid to do so.

Perhaps an illustration might help us to understand. An ocean liner leaves New York bound for Liverpool. Its destination has been determined by proper authorities. Nothing can change it. This is at least a faint picture of sovereignty.

On board the liner are scores of passengers. These are not in chains, neither are their activities determined for them by decree.

They are completely free to move about as they will. They eat, they sleep, play, lounge about on the deck, read, talk, altogether as they please; but all the while the great liner is carrying them steadily onward toward a predetermined port.

Both freedom and sovereignty are present here and they do not contradict each other. So it is, I believe, with man's freedom and the sovereignty of God. The mighty liner of God's sovereign design keeps its steady course over the sea of history. God moves undisturbed and unhindered toward the fulfillment of those eternal purposes which He purposed in Christ Jesus before the world began. We do not know all that is included in these purposes, but enough has been disclosed to furnish us with a broad outline of things to come and to give us good hope and firm assurance of future well-being.[1]

As children of God, our greatest desire should be to do His will. And in our most thoughtful, mature moments, we want to do His will. In fact, we delight in doing His will. And invariably, looking back, we are so grateful for the way He has led us thus far; we are amazed as we see how He has guided us to where He wanted us to be.

And that's what being on the ocean liner of God's will boils down to: going where He wants us to go and being what He wants us to be. This means releasing our own plans and pride and will as we flesh out His plan and purpose. That's what it's all about. In the process, we experience a deep inner peace, a satisfying sense of fulfillment, because we are within the circumference of His plan, moving inexorably toward His destined arrangement for our lives.

In the course of that plan we come under the decreed will of God, which generally covers the things revealed in the Scriptures and leaves unstated the things yet future. We participate in the specific parts of His will wherein we play a part. The latter is where the struggle often comes, because the process of God's will is not passive. It isn't a matter of just lying back and waiting for Him to move us from Plan A to Plan B.

For example, on a very mundane level, you're dressed today

because you dressed yourself this morning. You're full because you fed yourself that last meal. You are clean because you bathed yourself or took a shower. You got to work because you put gas in your car and drove yourself to your place of employment. You arrived on time because you take seriously the responsibilities that are part of your job profile. And had you simply stayed in bed, God would have done none of those things for you.

We cannot assume a slothful attitude that says, "God does it all, and if He wants this done, He'll have to do it." There are times, of course, when we reach a point where we must say, "I now must leave this in God's hands." But that is about coming to terms with what He wants rather than what I want.

In the previous chapter we affirmed that following the will of God requires faith and action, which in turn call for risk and release. This is where things get very personal; this is where we persevere and flesh out the will of God.

I have come to this conclusion: Doing the will of God is rarely easy and uncomplicated. Instead, it is often difficult and convoluted. Or, back to my preferred term, it is *mysterious.* Because we don't know where He is taking us, we must bend our wills to His—and most of us are not all that excited about bending. We'd much prefer resisting. That's why the Christian life is often such a struggle. I don't mean that it's a constant marathon of misery. It's just a struggle between our will and His will. Someday, when we are caught up with the Lord in glory, we will finally be all the things we have longed to be. Until then, we live in this never-ending tension of give and take, push and pull.

At the fork of every road, we need faith and action to follow God's leading. That is the crisis of belief that I mentioned at the end of the previous chapter. It is a turning point, where we must make a decision. It's like those expressway signs that say "Garden Grove Freeway, East, West," with arrows pointing to the two exit lanes. You're rolling along carefree at sixty-five miles an hour and suddenly you have to decide: Which way? East? West? Which is it? Only one way will get you where you want to go. So you have to make a decision. You can try to go in both directions, but it will hurt.

Jonah experienced that kind of crisis of belief when God told him to "Go to Nineveh." Although he was a prophet of God, his prejudice and bigotry got in the way of God's will for him. Nineveh was the capital of Assyria. Jonah despised the Ninevites because they were pagans, filled with idolatry and violence. "Go and proclaim my message there," God told Jonah. His map was clearly marked; God had told him which way to go. But Jonah still had to make a decision—to obey God or not. Jonah thought, "No way," and took the next ship to Tarshish, which was in the opposite direction, which is kind of like living in Texas and going to Berlin by way of Honolulu. (Tempting, isn't it?).

God refused to ignore the prophet's disobedience. He threw a few obstacles in his way—like a violent storm and a near-death experience in the belly of a fish—and gave Jonah another chance.

Jonah was vomited out of the fish, and while he was lying there gasping for breath on the beach, God repeated His will: "Go to Nineveh."

Another person who struggled with a crisis of belief was Sarah, Abraham's wife. "You will have a baby," God promised. Many years passed but she didn't conceive. Finally, she decided to take control of her own destiny. She told Abraham, "Go in to my handmaiden, Hagar, and have the child by her." Dumb decision. Instead of waiting for God's plan and timing, she rushed ahead and pushed Hagar into Abraham's tent. And to complicate things, Abraham foolishly cooperated. The result was Ishmael, and we all know where that led. The conflict that resulted between the descendants of Ishmael and the descendants of Isaac has only intensified through the centuries. Today the Arabs and the Jews are still in conflict with each other.

"To get from where you are to where God is will require major adjustments," writes Henry Blackaby. "These adjustments may relate to your thinking, circumstances, relationships, commitments, actions, and/or beliefs." To this list I would add geography, both physical and spiritual, because, as Blackaby warns, "you cannot stay where you are and go with God at the same time."[2]

It's at this point that we feel the vice tightening a little bit, and a subtle uneasiness sets in. *Well, what about my family?* we think. *What about my mom? She really needs me nearby.* Or, *I've finally found a great church. I don't want to leave this area.*

My mind flashes back to Tom and Sue Kimber, who were a part of our Insight for Living ministry for many years. Then one summer they decided to participate in a short internship in China. While there, they began to wonder, *Is this what God wants us to do? Is this where He wants us to be?* They loved Southern California; their family was there and their church was there. Besides, they didn't know one word of Chinese. Would God really call them and their son, Thomas, to such a distant place and unfamiliar culture?

Well, to cut to the chase, He did. And that's where they are today. Living in a culture that is totally unfamiliar. Reaching out to people who speak a different language. I can hardly imagine a greater adjustment for a couple and their son. But guess what? They are having the time of their lives. Because they made the right turn at the fork in the road, with a terrific attitude, they deliberately released and risked and got on with God's plan and process for their lives.

You may wonder how they could have done it. Easy answer . . . hard to apply: That's where faith comes into the equation. "And without faith it is impossible to please Him, for he who comes to God must believe that He is, and that He is a rewarder of those who seek Him" (Hebrews 11:6).

Faith is believing God is who He says He is and that He will do what He says He will do. Faith is obeying the Lord when I'm unsure of the outcome. Faith is trusting Him when everything in me screams for empirical proof: "Show it to me. Give me the evidence. I want it in a test tube. Put it under a microscope. Prove this. I need the whole picture clearly developed. When I see it, then I'll go with it."

God wants us to walk by faith, not by sight. But we're only comfortable when we can see what's ahead, and what's behind, and what's all around us. We want proof. We want guarantees. That's why we like contracts. Put it in writing, we say; I want a guarantee. We much prefer sight to faith. Extreme faith gives most Christians a rash.

We prefer talk to action. We can talk about the will of God for hours, just so we don't have to do it. While we may not admit it, we secretly cling to the familiar—we're not about to release it. We like the predictable rather than the risky. But God says, "If you're going to please Me, you're going to have to take My Word on this. You're going to have to believe that I am who I say I am, and that I will do what I say I will do." Plain and simple, we gag on that statement!

Seldom do we read the word "impossible" in Scripture. But here God says, "Without faith, pleasing Him is impossible."

God loves it when we trust Him without needing a panoramic picture before us. But trusting Him doesn't guarantee ease and simplicity. Living out the will of God can be difficult and convoluted. Sometimes we are literally at a loss to know what God is up to; but we know that staying where we are is not His plan. That is a tough place to be, because we know He is up to something, we want to be engaged in it, and we find ourselves restless, trying to figure it out. We're back to the mystery of God's will.

Fortunately, God has given us many examples of men and women who lived by faith, not by sight. These are historic models of faith and action, release and risk. They also prepare us for some of the difficulties we will encounter when we flesh out the will of God in our lives.

DOING GOD'S WILL MAY UPSET OTHERS

Hebrews 11, sometimes known as the roll call of faith, records at least a dozen people who modeled faith and action, release and risk. I'd like to look at four of them who offer realistic examples of people who did God's will by faith but found that it was not easy or comfortable or simple. The first is Abel.

By faith Abel offered to God a better sacrifice than Cain, through which he obtained the testimony that he was righteous, God testifying about his gifts, and through faith, though he is dead, he still speaks. (Hebrews 11:4)

Cain and Abel were sons of Adam and Eve. Abel was a shepherd, and Cain was a farmer. Both brought offerings to God. Cain brought some of his crops, but Abel brought the very best portions from his flock. One commentator says, "The contrast is not between an offering of plant life and an offering of animal life, but between a careless, thoughtless offering and a choice, generous offering. Motivation and heart attitude are all-important, and God looked with favor on Abel and his offering because of Abel's faith." [3]

Infuriated that God had accepted his brother's offering and not his own, Cain violently murdered his brother.

Sometimes when you do the will of God, you will upset or anger your family. This can result in great pressure, relational turmoil, angry words, and perhaps even hostile reactions against you. But remember, you are not on this earth as a child of God to please your family members.

I should also add, however, that we're not here deliberately to make our family members nervous. Motivation has to be the balance wheel here. But of the two, we want to be so committed to our heavenly Father that we know clearly and distinctly what His plan is. We're not here specifically to please our sons and daughters or our mothers and fathers. Sometimes our family can be wrong.

I know this from personal experience. Over forty-five years ago, my parents were not convinced that Cynthia was the best mate for me. They were sincere . . . but on that matter, they were wrong. Had I listened to them, I would not have married the woman I should have married. (We recently celebrated our forty-fourth wedding anniversary. It's still working!)

Now, if they are believers and if they're walking with the Lord, parents are usually good counselors on most things. But they don't walk on water. Sometimes parents can be shortsighted and selfish. This is also true of other family members, and sometimes your immediate family represents the most difficult part of your obeying the will of God. They may even become resentful or angry when they disagree with your life decisions. But when a crisis of belief occurs, faith and obedience must prevail. Releasing and risking will be required. First and foremost, we are to do God's will. That's Obedience 101.

Parents, here's a direct word for you at this point: We have two primary jobs as parents: (1) rearing our children carefully and (2) then releasing them completely. Children don't need our constant oversight or advice when they are grown. Cynthia and I have learned the hard way that our grown children receive our advice best when they ask us for it. At times, we have advice nobody's asking for; we have answers to questions nobody's asking. So we just wait for them to ask. Sometimes they do; often they don't. That's part of parenting, and admittedly, it's a tough part because no matter how old your children are, you don't stop worrying or caring, especially when you think they may be making a wrong decision. But again, faith not sight is what works here. Just turn them over to the Lord and rest in the confidence that He is working out His plan for their lives, just as He is working out His plan for yours.

DOING GOD'S WILL MAY LEAD TO A SURPRISE ENDING

Enoch is the next example of faith. The author of Hebrews says of him: "By faith Enoch was taken up so that he should not see death; *And He was not found because God took him up*; for he obtained the witness that before his being taken up he was pleasing to God" (Hebrews 11:5).

In Genesis 5 we learn that when Enoch was sixty-five years old, he had a son, Methuselah. And from then on, Enoch "walked with God." He walked with God for three hundred years, and "then he was no more, because God took him away." Surprisingly, the man was taken into the presence of God without ever experiencing death.

Now three hundred and sixty-five years may not seem like an early death to us, but in comparison to the length of time people lived in those days (Enoch's son Methuselah lived nine hundred and sixty-nine years), Enoch was a young man when God took him.

Sometimes a remarkable life of obedience is underscored by a premature death. In the mid-1950s, five young men felt God leading them to evangelize the Auca Indians in Ecuador. Jim Elliott, Nate Saint, Roger Youderian, Ed McCully, and Peter Fleming set out on this mission to take the good news of salvation to this hostile tribe of headhunters. All five of the men were found in or near the Curaray River with spears through their bodies. Nearby sat their destroyed plane, like a large bird that had invaded the enemy territory and threatened this tribe. The Aucas didn't understand that these men meant them no harm, nor that they had slaughtered five godly men. Later, Elisabeth Elliott, the widow of Jim Elliot, along with their young daughter and Rachel Saint, sister of the pilot, Nate Saint, returned to this place full of gruesome memories for them and led the very people who had killed their loved ones to the Lord.

In January 1958, I was a young Marine, resentful and disillusioned because I had to go overseas. I was visiting my brother Orville in Pasadena, California, and as I was preparing to return to Camp Pendleton, just prior to getting on the troop ship, Orville said to me, "Charles, here's a book I want you to read."

"I'm not interested in reading." I said.

"I didn't ask if you're interested in reading. I want you to read this book."

"I'm not gonna read the book."

He shoved it in my seabag and said, "Once you start, you'll never be able to put it down."

Later, I sat on the bus, looking out the rain-splattered window at the cold, wet January day. I was lonely, disillusioned, disappointed, and a little despairing of life. The Marine Corps didn't allow wives to accompany their husbands overseas, so Cynthia was back in Houston. How could God allow my wife and me to be separated like this? Turning away from the depressing scenery, and trying to turn away from my depressing thoughts, I pulled out the book my brother had given me.

The book was titled *Through Gates of Splendor,* and the author was Elisabeth Elliott. In it she told the story of those five men and their call to the Aucas. Reading that book absolutely transformed my thinking. My brother was correct. I couldn't put it down. When I got back to Camp Pendleton, I sat in the men's room reading, which was the only place on base that had lights through the night. I sat there all night reading until I finished the book. On the troop ship, seventeen days at sea, I read it again. And while stationed on Okinawa I read it a third time.

Through the years, I've had the privilege of meeting most of the widows of those five men and heard them tell the story, with tears in their eyes. And I've told Elisabeth Elliott that it was that book, and through it the witness of those men, that God used to turn my heart toward ministry and missions. Who knows how many other tens of thousands have been affected by the lives of those five young men whose faith was so deep that they walked with God until He said, "You come on home with Me now."

As I think of this, I think of another young man, Kris Boring, who graduated as one of our top students at Dallas Seminary. Kris was valedictorian of his high school class, top of his class in college, and a splendid student at the seminary. In May of 1997 I handed him his Master of Theology degree at commencement. Kris and his fiancée, thinking God's plan was for them to serve Him on the mission field, went together to look into a particular ministry opportunity. While there, Kris contracted a virus, and in two and a half weeks he was dead. Kris was twenty-eight years old.

I remember his saying to me after graduation, "I just can't wait. Now I can go. I'm all prepared." And surprisingly . . . mysteriously, God took him.

Who knows how many people, because of Kris Boring's premature death, will suddenly be made aware of God's plan for them. I don't know. I can't figure such things out. It's another mystery. But modern-day Enochs like Jim Elliott and Kris Boring still walk with God—and God takes them for *His* purposes.

Sometimes a person's life of obedience is underscored by a premature death. Remember this when it comes close to home. It will help you resist the questions "Why?" and "How could you, Lord?"

While attending Kris's memorial service I heard one student after another tell how this young man's death had riveted into them the importance of serving Christ with even greater devotion. Who knows if they would have seen the will of God so clearly if Kris had not been taken? All I know is that "Precious in the sight of the LORD is the death of His godly ones" (Psalm 116:15).

DOING GOD'S WILL MAY MEAN PERSECUTION

Our next model of faith and action, release and risk, is Noah.

> By faith Noah, being warned by God about things not yet seen, in reverence prepared an ark for the salvation of his household, by which he condemned the world, and became an heir of the righteousness which is according to faith. (Hebrews 11:7)

Noah was not just an ark builder. Before the flood, he was "a preacher of righteousness," and a man who "found favor in the eyes of the Lord" (2 Peter 2:5; Genesis 6:8).

Between the time God told Noah there would be a flood and the first sprinkles of rain, one hundred and twenty years elapsed. So for almost a century and a quarter—that's longer than any of us will live—Noah was building the ark and preparing for God's judgment.

> Then the LORD saw that the wickedness of man was great on the earth, and that every intent of the thoughts of his heart was only evil continually. (Genesis 6:5)

But Noah was different. He was sensitive to God; he heard God's message. God informed Noah of His plan: He was going to destroy the world with a flood. So for one hundred and twenty years, by faith, Noah followed the Lord's leading. He gathered the materials, he built the ark, probably to the ridicule of everyone around him. After all, this was a world that had never known rain; the earth was watered from beneath. And while Noah was building this ark, he was preaching righteousness to those around him. "The flood's coming, judgment's coming." Surrounded and mocked by his depraved, reprobate, wicked contemporaries, this preacher of righteousness, by faith, stood against the tide of his culture. Sometimes our faith is such a rebuke to our peers that we suffer persecution because of it. No extra charge for this simple warning: Don't expect overwhelming approval and affirmation just because you've chosen to walk by faith. History is replete with examples.

Back in the fourteenth century, there was a distinguished professor of divinity at Oxford University who, because of his faith, was "branded an instrument of the devil . . . the author of schism." He was driven into virtual exile by the hypocritical alliance of church and state authorities in the Roman Catholic Church, prompted by the pope's decision. I'm referring, of course, to John Wycliffe, once the pride of Oxford University, the foremost scholar of his day (according to more than one biographer), and clearly the most influential preacher in England at that time. Yet he could no longer stay in his ivory tower of academia knowing that the papacy was corrupt and the people were left in ignorance with no Bible in their own language.

We cannot fathom that. Our shelves are full of a multitude of versions and paraphrases of the Scripture in our own language and countless other languages, in every conceivable type size and binding and format. But in those days there was not one copy of the Bible in English. It was available only in the language of the clergy, Latin, and those were chained to the pulpits of the cathedrals. Unable to read God's Word for themselves, the people were at the mercy of the church leaders, who often relied on the people's ignorance in order to manipulate the public.

Wycliffe said, "This is not right. People should be able to read the Bible in their own language." And like Noah, who drove those nails into that ark while people mocked and scorned him, Wycliffe began the task of translating the Scriptures as a flood of persecution rose around him. He was publicly branded a heretic. When he finally finished the translation of the Scriptures, he wrote these words in the fly-leaf of the first copy of the English Scriptures: "This Bible is translated and shall make possible a government of the people, by the people, and for the people."[4] (Five hundred years later the sixteenth president of the United States, Abraham Lincoln, would borrow that statement for his great Gettysburg Address.)

Thirty years after Wycliffe's death he was again declared a heretic. As a result, his body was exhumed, the bones were burned to dust, and his ashes were cast into a river. A contemporary historian describes the scene like this:

> They burnt his bones to ashes and cast them into Swift, a neighboring brook running hard by. Thus this brook hath conveyed his ashes into (the river) Avon, Avon into Severn, Severn into the narrow seas, they into the main ocean. And thus ashes of Wicliffe are the emblem of his doctrine, which now are dispersed the world over.[5]

In a similar vein, Harry Emerson Fosdick writes these eloquent words: "His enemies, who thought they had now finished him, did not foresee history's verdict: "The Avon to the Severn runs, / And Severn to the sea; / And Wycliffe's dust shall spread abroad / Wide as the waters be.""[6]

Right now, your life of faith, lived in a culture of contemporary depravity, may not seem all that significant. Living out your faith at the office or in that university dorm or in your high school may feel pretty lonely. Walking by faith and honoring the Lord in your factory or in your profession or in the military may seem futile at times. In fact, in your own lifetime, you may never know the significance of your walk of faith. But God will use you in His special plan for your life, just as he did John Wycliffe and countless others.

I've sat in the castle where Luther hid while he was translating the Scriptures into the German vernacular. I've looked out his window and thought about Luther as he sat in that very room, faithfully discharging his task, knowing that if the church leaders found him they would put him to death. Wycliffe, Luther, Calvin, Savonarola, Knox, Wesley, Whitefield, Edwards . . . on and on the list goes, right up to today. While the world mocked, God honored them. And that still happens.

Just because something is God's will doesn't mean people will understand. On the contrary, most never do. But that's part of the mystery. Faith leads to action, requiring release and risk.

DOING GOD'S WILL MEANS
LEAVING THE FAMILIAR FOR THE UNKNOWN

Few epitomize "leaving the familiar" more than Abraham.

> By faith Abraham, when he was called, obeyed by going out to a place which he was to receive for an inheritance; and he went out, not knowing where he was going. By faith he lived as an alien in the land of promise, as in a foreign land, dwelling in tents with Isaac and Jacob, fellow heirs of the same promise; for he was looking for the city which has foundations, whose architect and builder is God. (Hebrews 11:8–10)

Abraham had lived all of his life in Ur of the Chaldeans, as had his father before him. He had deep, long roots in that place. Then, when he was seventy-five-years old (think of it!), God told Abraham to leave his homeland for a "land which I will show you" (Genesis 12:1).

There he is, getting on in years, and he and his wife, Sarah, who is only ten years younger than he is, have settled into their comfortable life together. Suddenly God comes along and invades their nest. His will is clearly stated: "Move out!"

Now, picture the scene: Abraham and Sarah have no children, but they do have a lot of family and friends. And one day Abraham announces to all of them, "We're moving."

"At your age?" they say. "Why would you do that?"

"Well, God told us."

"Right. So where are you going?"

"Well, He hasn't told us that." (Just imagine the reaction).

So they load up the camels and pile everything they own on the carts and start making their way out of Ur. The biblical account makes it clear: Abraham went out "not knowing where he was going" (Heb. 11:8).

Abraham was a relatively wealthy man, and now he found himself dwelling in a tent, living like an alien, because "he was looking for the city which has foundations, whose architect and builder is God" (Heb. 11:10). (I love that description).

Out of the blue, with no details provided, God said, "Go, and I'll show you where later." And Abraham obeyed by going out, "not knowing where he was going." Talk about releasing and risking.

I'm reminded of John Henry Jowett's comment, "Ministry that costs nothing, accomplishes nothing."[7] Remember that, in this era of cheap grace. In fact, I suggest you memorize that line: "Ministry that costs nothing, accomplishes nothing."

Abraham paid the price of comfort and familiarity in order to do the will of God. This is a classic example of the crisis of belief and the need for major adjustment, of faith and action, release and risk.

Discovering and then obeying God's will may require you to leave the familiar and the comfortable.

In my friend Warren Wiersbe's book *Walking with the Giants,* one of the giants he writes about is Hudson Taylor, another of our heroes of faith.

A Presbyterian moderator in a Melbourne, Australia, church used all his eloquence to introduce the visiting missionary speaker, finally presenting him to the congregation as "our illustrious guest." He was not prepared for James Hudson Taylor's first sentence: "Dear friends, I am the little servant of an illustrious Master."

Nearly twenty years before, Hudson Taylor had written in an editorial, "All God's giants have been weak men, who did great things for God because they reckoned on His being with them." As he looked at himself, Hudson Taylor saw nothing but weakness; but as generations of Christians have studied Taylor's life, they have become acquainted with a man who dared to believe the Word of God and, by faith, carried the gospel to inland China—and saw God work wonders![8]

"Want of trust," said Hudson Taylor, "is at the root of almost all our sins and all our weaknesses."[9]

The man was thirty-three when he founded China Inland Mission on June 27, 1865. In doing so, he was the first to take the gospel to the people of that land. Leaving his familiar, comfortable homeland in England, he walked with God as an alien in a land that God had placed on his heart.

Discovering and embracing God's will invariably brings us to a crisis of belief. And that forces us into faith and action.

Obeying and delighting in God's will leads us to make major adjustments. And that requires us to release and risk—releasing the familiar and risking whatever the future may bring. That's the bottom line of fleshing out God's will.

The longer we walk with the Lord, the more we realize that we really don't know what each new day may bring. A phone call can come in the middle of the night shattering our joy. Suddenly, everything changes. It's amazing what a knock at the door can bring or what the opening of a letter can do.

I don't say these things to conjure up fear in our hearts, but simply to remind us that God alone knows our future. And there's no safer, no better, no more rewarding place to be than in the nucleus of His will, regardless of where that may be.

In spite of all our struggling, there's something within us, down in our redeemed hearts, that craves to know His smile, His rewards, and the joy of following obedience. Nothing can be compared to that. No salary offers it; no money can buy it; no possession can replace it . . . just knowing we have pleased our Father is sufficient.

God is not running around hiding from us, mocking us, or delighting in keeping us squirming in a dungeon of confusion. In many ways, His will for us emerges very clearly as we go through this process we've been considering. But we do have to be willing to walk by faith, which means doing His will against seemingly insurmountable odds.

We are only finite human beings. We can only see the present and the past. The future is a little frightening to us. So we need to hold onto His hand and trust Him to calm our fears. And at those times when we're stubborn and resisting and God shakes us by the shoulders to get our attention, we're reminded that we don't call our own shots, that God has a plan for us, mysterious though it may seem, and we want to be in the center of it.

All the risks notwithstanding, that is still the safest place on earth to be.

5

Another Deep Mystery: God's Sovereignty

Let us then learn the rule and the order, which God is in
the habit of using in the government of the saints. For I,
too, have frequently tried to prescribe certain methods
for God to employ in the administration either of the
church or of other affairs. Ah, Lord, said I, I should like
to have this matter done in this way, in this order, and
with this result . . . But God did the very opposite of
what I asked.

—MARTIN LUTHER, *What Luther Says*

In many ways, you still want to set your own agenda.
You act as if you have to choose among many things,
which all seem equally important. But you have not fully
surrendered yourself to God's guidance.
You keep fighting with God over who is in control.

—HENRI NOUWEN, *The Inner Voice of Love*

Control is an illusion, you infantile egomaniac!
Nobody controls anything.

—Nicole Kidman to Tom Cruise in *Days of Thunder*

Chapter Five

❧

Another Deep Mystery: God's Sovereignty

In the summer of 1961 my life was changed. I was already a Christian. In fact, I was between my second and third year in seminary, deeply entrenched in theological studies. I had been invited to intern that summer at a church in Northern California, Peninsula Bible Church, which I did, along with another young man named Gib Martin. During that three-month period, Gib, still single at the time, lived with Cynthia and me.

I was struggling with some of the more profound truths in the Word of God during those days. When you're in graduate study and are doing intensive work in the biblical text, you must wrestle with and to come to terms with certain truths. You can no longer leave them in the "unsettled" realm. One of my major battles at the time was the sovereignty of God.

Candidly, this doctrine frightened me. In seminary I had seen some close friends take God's sovereignty to such ridiculous extremes that they had become unbalanced . . . in my mind, borderline heretical.

On a practical level, I was grappling with several issues in my own life that seemed to relate. Cynthia and I were uncertain about our future. We had been married for over six years, and while our marriage was not weak, it wasn't as strong as it needed to be. And she was carrying our first child, causing both of us to feel somewhat anxious about being parents. Neither of us had come from homes where we had great parenting models to follow. They were good homes and we were loved, but much of the parenting process was lacking, at least from our perspective.

All of this, as well as a few other issues, were troubling me. So that summer I decided I really wanted to dig into a book of the Bible, ideally one with a dozen chapters or so to coincide with the twelve weeks that we would be away from school. I chose the Book of Daniel. I had never seriously studied the book on my own, so I decided to spend a major portion of my morning devotional time in each week's given chapter. It was in our fourth week at Peninsula Bible Church in Palo Alto, California, when I was in the fourth chapter of Daniel, that I came upon the truth that transformed my thinking and, in fact, changed my life.

To give you a little background, Daniel 4 begins with a dialogue and ends with a monologue. The chapter revolves around a dream. Nebuchadnezzar, the king of Babylon, had a dream that disturbed him. None of his wise men could interpret the dream for him, so he ended up consulting a Jewish prophet named Daniel. Daniel not only interpreted the dream; he also exhorted the dreamer.

Nebuchadnezzar was a proud man, a heavy-handed ruler; all he had to do was turn thumbs down and Daniel's life would be history. He was the sovereign monarch of Babylon, humanly speaking. But Daniel had the divine courage to look Nebuchadnezzar in the eye, as all true prophets would do, and tell him the truth. As he interpreted the dream, he challenged King Nebuchadnezzar to do something about the truth that it represented.

This is the interpretation, O king, and this is the decree of the Most High, which has come upon my lord the king: that you be driven away from mankind, and your dwelling place be with the beasts of the field, and you be given grass to eat like cattle and be drenched with the dew of heaven; and seven periods of time will pass over you, until you recognize that the Most High is ruler over the realm of mankind, and bestows it on whomever He wishes.

And in that it was commanded to leave the stump with the roots of the tree, your kingdom will be assured to you after you recognize that it is Heaven that rules.

Therefore, O king, may my advice be pleasing to you: break away now from your sins by doing righteousness, and from your iniquities by showing mercy to the poor, in case there may be a prolonging of your prosperity.'

All this happened to Nebuchadnezzar the king.
(Daniel 4:24–28)

A chill still runs up my spine when I read these words and reflect back on that summer morning in Palo Alto. I remember, as if it were yesterday, taking a pencil from my desk and underscoring two lines that are almost identical. In verse 25, "until you recognize," and verse 26, "after you recognize."

In essence, Daniel says, "All of this will happen to you, Nebuchadnezzar, *until* you recognize that you aren't sovereign over your life, *until* you recognize that the Most High is the ruler. Things will not change until *after* you recognize that it is Heaven that rules."

Recognize. The Hebrew verb is "know." Perhaps the word "acknowledge" is a better translation than "recognize." And the NIV renders it so: "until you acknowledge." You can recognize something and not be involved in it. But you can't really acknowledge something without having some kind of involvement and acceptance—even embracing. I think that's what Daniel has in mind. "Nebuchadnezzar, until you embrace the truth that you aren't sovereign, but God is . . . that you don't rule your life, but God does, you will never break from that insane experience."

Stop and think for a moment about the word "sovereignty." There's a smaller word nestled in the heart of it, the word "reign": sov-*reign*-ty.

Nebuchadnezzar conducted his life as if he were reigning over it, just like he reigned over his kingdom. Then Daniel steps on the scene and says, "God has given you this dream so that you will know that there is another way of viewing life: The eternal God of heaven, your creator, not only made you and gives you breath for your lungs, but He *reigns* over you." This must have been a tough pill for Nebuchadnezzar to swallow.

Now notice the first three words in the next verse:

Twelve months later he was walking on the roof of the royal palace of Babylon. (Daniel 4:29, italics mine)

"Twelve months later." A full year has passed, during which God has patiently allowed Nebuchadnezzar to let that truth wash around in his mind. "Do I reign over my life or does the Creator? Am I sovereign or is He? Is He in control? Are His ways being carried out? Or am I in control, accomplishing my ways?"

Well, his answer emerges in the following verses.

The king reflected and said, "Is this not Babylon the great, which I myself have built as a royal residence by the might of my power and for the glory of my majesty?"

While the word was in the king's mouth, a voice came from heaven, saying, "King Nebuchadnezzar, to you it is declared: sovereignty has been removed from you, and you will be driven away from mankind, and your dwelling place will be with the beasts of the field. You will be given grass to eat like cattle, and seven periods of time will pass over you, until you recognize that the Most High is ruler over the realm of mankind, and bestows it on whomever He wishes."

Immediately the word concerning Nebuchadnezzar was fulfilled; and he was driven away from mankind and began eating grass like cattle, and his body was drenched with the dew of heaven, until his hair had grown like eagles' feathers and his nails like birds' claws. (Daniel 4:30–33)

Nebuchadnezzar went completely insane. He literally lived out in the fields. Totally removed from the realm of logic and reason, this once-proud sovereign of the land lived in the wilderness like a beast.

But the story isn't over. And this is where the dialogue between Daniel and the king becomes a monologue. I think Daniel gave Nebuchadnezzar the pen and said, "Here, you write the rest of this story."

But at the end of that period I, Nebuchadnezzar, raised my eyes toward heaven, and my reason returned to me, and I blessed the Most High and praised and honored Him who lives forever;

> For His dominion is an everlasting dominion,
> And His kingdom endures from generation to generation.
> And all the inhabitants of the earth are accounted as nothing,
> But He does according to His will in the host of heaven
> And among the inhabitants of earth;
> And no one can ward off His hand
> Or say to Him, "What hast Thou done?"

At that time my reason returned to me. And my majesty and splendor were restored to me for the glory of my kingdom, and my counselors and my nobles began seeking me out; so I was reestablished in my sovereignty, and surpassing greatness was added to me.

Now I Nebuchadnezzar praise, exalt, and honor the King of heaven, for all His works are true and His ways just, and He is able to humble those who walk in pride. (Daniel 4:34–37)

I vividly recall that morning in Palo Alto when I circled six statements in these verses. Verse 34: "His dominion" and "His kingdom." Verse 35: "His will" and "His hand." Verse 37: "His works" and "His ways." Everything the king had experienced and everything that followed his insanity was of God. *All* orchestrated by God, alone.

I sat and stared at that passage of Scripture for who knows how long. My heart beat faster, and I broke out in a sweat as I struggled with what I had read. Finally I told the Lord that I would give up the fight and acquiesce to His plan. I invited Him to take sovereign charge of my life. I gave Him my marriage. I gave Him my wife. I gave Him the birth of our firstborn. In fact, I surrendered my entire future to Him. And I finished the time on my knees weeping in wonder and with a sense of relief. From then on, it would be "God, and God alone."

I don't write this story to sound dramatic or pious; I tell you this story because it changed my life. And I would need a reminder of this moment several years later when Cynthia and I suffered through two miscarriages. The sovereignty of God came to my rescue in those tragic hours. I needed this reminder when we were involved in a terrible automobile collision that broke our son's jaw and injured my wife seriously and totaled our car on the icy streets of Houston. I needed this reminder during the hard times in the years that would follow in various struggles we have endured, from being misunderstood, misrepresented, and maligned. I need it today. Good times and hard times. Happiness and hardship. Gain and loss. Promotion and demotion. Joy and sorrow. Ecstasy and tragedy. Confusion and clarity. His sovereignty covers it all. God, and God alone, is in full control.

That summer morning in 1961, I decided my entire life would be His dominion and His kingdom, not mine. It would be His will shaped by His hand, not mine. It would be His works and His ways, not mine, that I would spend the balance of my life proclaiming and promoting. That decision, I repeat again, totally transformed my life.

I also promised Him that every chance I got when I had a chance to speak of His character, sovereignty would be first and foremost, and that by His grace I would be faithful in promoting that major doctrine every chance I got. Here's another chance to do so.

His way is always right. It doesn't always make sense—in fact, as we are learning, it is often mysterious. It can seldom be explained. It isn't always pleasurable and fun. But I have lived long enough to realize that His way is always right.

And that's what Nebuchadnezzar had to acknowledge. In fact, not until he acknowledged it did true reasoning return to him. Following this example, I believe that not until we embrace God's sovereignty will we have the ability to reason our way through life theologically. Until then we will be too important in the plan. Man's opinion will be too significant to us. And we will churn and wrestle and struggle our way through this Christian life, trying too hard to please people rather than living it relieved and relaxed in His plan.

ONLY GOD IS SOVEREIGN

Long before Daniel said those words to Nebuchadnezzar and Nebuchadnezzar wrote them for himself, God had led Solomon to write this proverb: "The king's heart is like channels of water in the hand of the Lord; He turns it wherever He wishes" (Proverbs 21:1).

Often, when looking upon great kings and great presidents and great governors and great men and women of state, we suck in our breath in awe. Yet God is able to move their hearts like His finger would reach down and retrace the course of a river. It's no problem to Him. He moves as He wills, and He isn't through doing so. Let me add, this isn't limited to kings. It's true of you and me.

Now that's hard to accept if you are a proud person, especially if that pride is connected with stubbornness. (Usually they go together.) You resist that thought because you can name some people who have gone through some awful times, and you say, "You're telling me that God smiled on *that?* He was responsible for *that?* He allowed *that?*" Yes, God, and God alone.

Although I have referred to him before, Job's situation bears repeating. Here was a man who lost everything but wife and life. As we saw earlier, He lost his children, his home, his livestock, his servants, his bankroll, everything! He even lost his health. His body was covered with oozing skin ulcers. You and I can't imagine such pain.

And on top of that, he had to listen to Eliphaz, Bildad, Zophar, and Elihu, his so-called friends, lecture him on why he was getting what he was due. Finally God breaks His silence and addresses Job personally. I would suggest that when you finish this chapter you read through the final five chapters of Job . . . but for now, glance over these highlights slowly and thoughtfully:

Then the LORD answered Job out of the whirlwind and said,

> Who is this that darkens counsel
> By words without knowledge?
> Now gird up your loins like a man,
> And I will ask you, and you instruct Me!
> Where were you when I laid the foundation of the earth?
> Tell Me, if you have understanding,
> Who set its measurements, since you know?
> Or who stretched the line on it?
> On what were its bases sunk?
> Or who laid its cornerstone,
> When the morning stars sang together,
> And all the sons of God shouted for joy?
>
> Or who enclosed the sea with doors,
> When, bursting forth, it went out from the womb;
> When I made a cloud its garment,
> And thick darkness its swaddling band,
> And I placed boundaries on it,
> And I set a bolt and doors,
> And I said, "Thus far you shall come, but no farther;
> And here shall your proud waves stop"?
>
> Have you ever in your life commanded the morning,
> And caused the dawn to know its place;
> That it might take hold of the ends of the earth,
> And the wicked be shaken out of it?

It is changed like clay under the seal;
And they stand forth like a garment.
And from the wicked their light is withheld,
And the uplifted arm is broken.

Have you entered into the springs of the sea?
Or have you walked in the recesses of the deep?
Have the gates of death been revealed to you?
Or have you seen the gates of deep darkness?
Have you understood the expanse of the earth?
Tell Me, if you know all this.

Where is the way to the dwelling of light?
And darkness, where is its place,
That you may take it to its territory,
And that you may discern the paths to its home?
You know, for you were born then,
And the number of your days is great!
Have you entered the storehouses of the snow,
Or have you seen the storehouses of the hail,
Which I have reserved for the time of distress,
For the day of war and battle?

(Job 38:1–23)

"Then the Lord answered Job out of the whirlwind." That's the way the Lord saw all the counsel Job had been getting before He appeared on the scene—a humanistic whirlwind. Ever been in a place like that? Ever been in a quandary and then you've had people volunteer their counsel and push their advice on you? Before very long it's all conflicting and confusing, anything but comforting. It's like a man-made *whirlwind!* And you long to hear God's clear, pristine message.

That's what Job finally gets. And what God says to Job is what we needed to hear: "I am in charge. I know what I'm doing. My way is right. Pain, suffering, and all, I am reigning sovereignly over you."

Then He asks Job a series of rhetorical questions that emphasize the fact that He, and He alone, is in control. Our newspapers report, "Disaster strikes! Blizzard sweeps across the north Midwest." And we say, "What a tragedy." God says, "I had My storehouses all ready and I sent the snow." Yes. Either that or He is *partially* sovereign . . . He is *almost* in control. Impossible. That's like my being *almost* a husband or *almost* a father.

God then talks about the stars, the constellations above us. Do we have any control over that? No, we can make lenses that help us see them, but we can't change the direction of the stars. We can stand back in amazement, and study the heavenly patterns, but we can't change the movement or alter the order of the universe.

Throughout these chapters, God addresses many of the other parts of His creation, until finally Job hears enough.

> Then Job answered the Lord, and said,
> "I know that Thou canst do all things,
> And that no purpose of Thine can be thwarted."
> (Job 42:1–2)

Job got a four-year seminary education in a few fleeting moments with the living Lord! God kept piling it on, until finally Job says, "I've got it. I see it! It's clear . . . it's clear. No purpose of Thine can be thwarted."

"No purpose of Thine can be thwarted." Remember that conclusion. Don't scissor that out of your Bible. Mark it and memorize it. When God says it shall be done, it will be done. If it makes me unhappy? It makes me unhappy. If it hurts? It hurts. If it ruins my reputation? It ruins my reputation. God says it shall be done and His purpose will not be thwarted . . . or He is not sovereign.

You want to know who's in charge around here? The One who called the spaces into being, the One who put the clouds in place, the One who established the atmosphere in which we're able to live, the One who separated the seas and the dry land, who gave you breath for your lungs and the ability to think. The One who placed you here, now, in time, for His purpose, and the One who with the snap of His divine finger will pull you from life into eternity. Mysterious though our lives may seem, God, and God alone, is in charge.

Whoever is sovereign must have total, clear perspective. He must see the end from the beginning. He must have no match on earth or in heaven. He must entertain no fears, no ignorance, and have no needs. He must have no limitations and always know what is best. He must never make a mistake. He must possess the ability to bring everything to a purposeful conclusion and an ultimate goal. He must be invincible, immutable, infinite, and self-sufficient. His judgments must be unsearchable and His ways unfathomable. He must be able to create rather than invent, to direct rather than wish, to control rather than hope, to guide rather than guess, to fulfill rather than dream. Who qualifies? You guessed it . . . God, and God alone.

And that doesn't begin to describe His resumé. He is our God, the One who says "it shall be" and it is done, and "it shall not be" and it is held back.

William Wordsworth, in his poem "Prelude," describes how wonderful it was for him to escape the city where he had been pent up for so long. Now, he says, "I'm free, free as a bird to settle where I will."[1] Free as a bird?

One man put it this way: "The naturalist knows that the supposedly free bird actually lives its entire life in a cage made of fears, hungers, and instincts; it is limited by weather conditions, varying air pressures, the local food supply, predatory beasts, and that strangest of all bonds, the irresistible compulsion to stay within the small plot of land and air assigned it by birdland committee. The freeist bird is, along with every other created thing, held in constant check by a net of necessity. Only God is free."[2]

Certainly you and I know nothing of freedom. We are bound to a very particular planet with a very particular climate and set of conditions in which we can survive. We are bound by relationships.

Bound by gravity. Bound by nature. Relying on God for the very impulses that cause our hearts to beat and our lungs to breathe and our bodies to move and our brains to think. Free? We strut about as though we are free . . . what a joke! The fact of the matter is, we are incredibly dependent people, every one of us.

Only God knows no such dependence. Only He is sovereign.

WHAT IS SOVEREIGNTY?

The apostle Paul developed this topic as well as anyone in Romans 9–11, and I want to challenge you to make your own study of those chapters. And if you don't struggle with those chapters, you're not really studying them. You'll think you have it all solved in chapter 9, and then you'll come upon chapter 10, and you'll struggle with what was said in chapter 9. But when you finally come to that great doxology at the end of chapter 11, perhaps you will, as I did, sigh with a sense of incomprehensible relief, leaving much of the mystery with God. Remember the words? We looked at them earlier.

Oh, the depth of the riches both of the wisdom and knowledge of God! How unsearchable are His judgments and unfathomable His ways! (Romans 11:33)

Let's revisit the scene of this grand doxology. This brilliant apostle, under the direction of the Spirit of God, extols the Lord our Father as being full of wisdom and knowledge. So whatever is sovereign is bathed in wisdom and knowledge. When He makes His decisions, which here are called "judgments," they are "unsearchable," because we live in a finite realm and He in the infinite. We live in the temporal now. He lives in the eternal forever. So His decisions, His judgments are "unsearchable." Furthermore, His ways, while they are right, are in the final analysis "unfathomable." You cannot get to the bottom of them. You do, however, often come to the place where you say: "I just accept it." And that requires a humility that is very difficult for the educated, intelligent person of today.

All this has led me to a simple definition: Sovereignty means our all-wise, all-knowing God reigns in realms beyond our comprehension to bring about a plan beyond our ability to alter, hinder, or stop.

Let me go further. His plan includes all promotions and demotions. His plan can mean both adversity and prosperity, tragedy and calamity, ecstasy and joy. It envelops illness as much as health, perilous times as much as comfort, safety, prosperity, and ease. His plan is at work when we cannot imagine why, because it is so unpleasant, as much as when the reason is clear and pleasant. His sovereignty, though it is inscrutable, has dominion over all handicaps, all heartaches, all helpless moments. It is at work through all disappointments, broken dreams, and lingering difficulties. And even when we cannot fully fathom why, He knows. Even when we cannot explain the reasons, He understands. And when we cannot see the end, He is there, nodding, "Yes, that is My plan."

> For who has known the mind of the Lord, or who became His counselor? Or who has first given to him that it might be paid back to him again? For from Him and through Him and to Him are *all things*. To Him be the glory forever. Amen. (Romans 11:34–36)

If you want to alter sovereignty and make it temporal or limited, then you have to get rid of "all things," just as you must do in Romans 8:28.

> And we know that God causes *all things* to work together for good to those who love God, to those who are called according to His purpose. (Romans 8:28)

If God says "all things," He means just that.

And "all things" are for His glory forever. "To Him be the glory forever and ever." Our Sovereign is the master and the mover. He is the giver and the receiver. He is the originator, for it says "from Him." He is the enforcer, for it says "through Him." He is the provider, for it says "to Him are all things." And lest we think of this as a blind, bitter fate, remember, it is for His greater glory forever.

Right about now, some of you reading these words are getting really nervous. You've already begun to plan the letter you want to write this author, saying, "Chuck, I think you've gone off the deep end." Let me put your mind at ease. It was the madness of that kind of extremism that kept me from embracing sovereignty. That was why my own wrestling endured so long. And it isn't that I don't still wrestle with these things at times. Believe me, I do. But hear me on this: When people take this doctrine to unbiblical extremes, they become passive and uninvolved. They lack zeal, become irresponsible, and do not strive for personal excellence. All is of God, they say; so God does everything.

I find it interesting that the apostle who writes this grand three-chapter declaration and ends it on such a high note devotes the balance of the Book of Romans to *our* responsibilities. The doctrine of the book is chapters 1 through 11, but from chapter 12 on, it's mainly about duty. "God is in control," the apostle says. "God is in charge," "God is sovereign," "God is responsible." But then . . .

> I urge you therefore, brethren, by the mercies of God, to present your bodies a living and holy sacrifice, acceptable to God, which is your spiritual service of worship. (Romans 12:1)

This command is to the believer, and there's a sense of urgency about it. There's responsibility.

> And do not be conformed to this world, but be transformed by the renewing of your mind, that you may prove what the will of God is, that which is good and acceptable and perfect. (Romans 12:2)

You have a responsibility not to let the world around you squeeze you into its own mold. "Oh, don't worry about that. I believe in sovereignty." Well, so does the one who wrote it. And he says it's our responsibility to guard against that happening.

And since we have gifts that differ according to the grace given to us, let each exercise them accordingly: if prophecy, according to the proportion of his faith; if service, in his serving; or he who teaches, in his teaching; or he who exhorts, in his exhortation; he who gives, with liberality; he who leads, with diligence; he who shows mercy, with cheerfulness. (Romans 12:6–8)

Look at that! One command after another, one active imperative after another. And it goes on into chapter 13, and into chapter 14, and further into chapter 15.

God's sovereignty does not mean that I am released from responsibility. It does not mean I have no interest in today's affairs, or that I cannot be bothered about decisions, or that I need not concern myself with the eternal destiny of the lost. It doesn't mean that at all. Somehow there has to be a balance.

In his book *The Knowledge of the Holy,* A. W. Tozer writes these very wise words:

God sovereignly decreed that man should be free to exercise moral choice, and man from the beginning has fulfilled that decree by making his choice between good and evil. When he chooses to do evil, he does not thereby countervail the sovereign will of God but fulfills it, inasmuch as the eternal decree decided not which choice the man should make but that he should be free to make it. [3]

That choice, amazingly, includes our choice of destiny. I personally believe that our Lord God has given us the privilege of choice. We can choose *for* or we can choose *against.* But we cannot choose the consequences. If we choose against the person of Jesus Christ, we thereby step into God's decree of eternal punishment. If we choose in favor of the Lord Jesus Christ, then we inherit all the rewards of heaven—the blessing of forgiven sins and eternity with God. God rules. God reigns. And His way is right.

Where will all of this lead? "To Him be the glory forever. Amen." And don't think that most people think of that. Most of us think: How will I get the glory? What will be the benefits to me? How will I be blessed? In God's sovereign plan, your life may be painful, disappointing, difficult, inexplicably confusing, and downright mysterious. But through it all, God somehow will get all the glory.

I think of that when I read this:

> Then comes the end, when He delivers up the kingdom to the God and Father, when He has abolished all rule and all authority and power.
>
> For He must reign until He has put all His enemies under His feet.
>
> The last enemy that will be abolished is death.
>
> For *He has put all things in subjection under his feet.* But when He says, "All things are put in subjection," it is evident that He is excepted who put all things in subjection to Him.
>
> And when all things are subjected to Him, then the Son Himself also will be subjected to the One who subjected all things to Him, that God may be all in all. (1 Corinthians 15:24–28, italics mine)

We come all the way to the end of time, just before we step into eternity future. And God is setting forth the final plans for this earth and all of its inhabitants. I love this section because it's so final, so clear: "Then comes the end."

Is that great or what? And at the very end we read the ultimate objective: "that God may be all in all." That's what heaven's door will read. "God is all in all!" Even in tragedy? Even in tragedy. Even in loss? Even in loss. Even in joy and sorrow? Yes, even in all of that. Even in earthquakes? Yes. I don't know how. I don't know why. But even in calamity, even in your home that's been split apart, even there "all things are subjected to Him . . . that God may be all in all."

That's the last chapter of the Book:

> And there shall no longer be any curse; and the throne of God and of the Lamb shall be in it, and His bond-servants shall serve Him; and they shall see His face, and His name shall be on their foreheads.

And there shall no longer be any night; and they shall not have
need of the light of a lamp nor the light of the sun, because the Lord
God shall illumine them; and they shall reign forever and ever.
(Revelation 22:3–5)

God rules. God reigns. God, and God alone. And His way is
right. It leads to His glory.

Deep within the hearts of men and women, even though most
would never acknowledge it, is this realization that we really don't
have the final answer. There is this little hidden clause tucked away
in the deep recesses of most thinking minds that says, "There may be
a God after all."

When we take this to the ultimate future for humanity, God is
sovereignly in charge. One second after they die, the men and
women who have rejected and resisted the Lord for years will step
into eternity. One second . . . and they will be totally at a loss to
determine their future. God's sovereignty steps over their lives and
sets forth His decree, "That God may be all in all."

BUT WHAT DOES IT ALL MEAN?

God's sovereignty. A mysterious doctrine at times, but one with great
relevance for our lives. Not just something for scholars and theologians to argue over.

First of all, the sovereignty of God relieves me from anxiety. It doesn't
take away my questions. It takes away my anxiety. When I rest in it,
I am relieved of the worry.

Second, the sovereignty of God frees me from explanation. I don't
have to have all the answers. I find ease in saying to certain individuals at critical times, "You know, I don't know. I can't unravel His full
plan in this."

The problem with learning a little theology, remember, is that we
start thinking we can unscrew the inscrutable. Believing we can fathom
the unfathomable. That there's no depth that we cannot plumb. Well,

let's face it . . . that's not true. There are some times when those who know the most simply must back off with hands behind their back and say, "It's beyond me. I don't know why God closes some doors and opens others. I don't know why some reject Him and become vessels of wrath. I don't know how that fits in. I don't know how evil can be used for good. And I don't know how the interplay between the two in some way glorifies God. But I know ultimately it does and it will, because God will be all in all. I don't have to explain it.

Third, the sovereignty of God keeps me from pride. Once I got hold of that thought in 1961, it began to revisit me on a regular basis throughout the balance of my education and then on into ministry. I have returned to it again and again and again. And it's helped me face some of the most difficult times of my life. It's kept me on my face before God.

Like every other human being, I have many, many battles. I have numerous sins—recurring sins—that plague me. Sins I wrestle with and confess and bring before God. But I have to tell you, because of my firm confidence in the sovereignty of God, pride is not a major battle for me. I never think of being proud, not even secretly. Sovereignty solves that battle once and for all! Instead, I am grateful that He's given me breath and the ability to think and to minister and to serve.

He's sovereign over my life. And He's sovereign over your life. He's sovereign whether you accept it or not. Nebuchadnezzar discovered that fact. You may not know it right now, but you'll know it a second after you die. God, and God alone, rules. His way is right.

John Oxenham, back in 1613, called this "God's Handwriting."

> He writes in characters too grand
> For our short sight to understand;
> We catch but broken strokes, and try
> To fathom all the mystery
> Of withered hopes of death, of life,
> The endless war, the useless strife—
> But there, with larger, clearer sight,

We shall see this—
His way was right.
His way was right.[4]

After all these years, I am still so grateful for that epochal moment in the summer of 1961 when I was forced to come to terms with an issue that had been troubling me. I'm grateful for the comfort it has brought over the years. I'm satisfied that God was directly involved when my eyes fell upon that passage in Daniel. And I thank Him for preserving this account of King Nebuchadnezzar and of Job and the writings of Paul so that we might learn that His rule and His sovereignty is right. His way is right.

Sometimes we struggle. Sometimes the handwriting is difficult to read or hard to accept. But I pray that the Lord will minister in a very special way to you who are struggling, who are coming to terms with His right to rule over you. And I pray that the name of the almighty, sovereign God will be lifted up, and that all the glory will be His . . . despite the mystery of it all.

6

Reading God's Mysterious Lips

All is riddle, and the key to a riddle is another riddle.

—EMERSON, *The Conduct of Life*

In human intercourse the tragedy begins.
Not when there is misunderstanding about words,
but when silence is not understood.

—THOREAU, *A Week on the Concord and Merrimack Rivers*

I found Him in the shining of the stars,
I marked Him in the flowering of His fields,
But in His ways with men I find Him not.

—ALFRED, LORD TENNYSON, *Idylls of the King*

Chapter Six

⊱⊰

Reading God's Mysterious Lips

In the mid-1970s I had to have tympanoplasty surgery done on my right ear. I was born with a congenital hole in that ear, which, consequently, was susceptible to infection. During my childhood, I suffered some painful bouts with this, and by the time I reached my late thirties, the hole had gotten larger, which meant I was beginning to experience a slight loss of hearing. So my surgeon repaired the damage by using a little bit of my fascia, which is located immediately under the scalp, to rebuild my eardrum.

Tympanoplasty is not a painful surgery, but it does require a somewhat lengthy recovery time. And while I was recovering, I thought quite a bit about what life would be like without hearing. What would be the difficulties, the major adjustments? I decided that one major adjustment would be learning to read lips.

I remembered this last year when I was speaking at a conference and a woman, who always sat on the front row, came up and thanked me for articulating carefully. "I can't hear, so I have learned to read lips," she said. When I asked if this was very difficult for her, she said, "Oh no . . . I watch television, I go to movies, I do all the things that many people think those without hearing could never do." And then she added this insightful thought: "It's great, actually. I really get to study the person who is speaking, really get to watch closely, because I can't take my eyes off the lips. If I do, I don't hear what's going on."

All this ties in beautifully with our walk with the Lord, for God is not only invisible and sovereign, He is also silent. Some of the great hymn writers have scripted eloquent lyrics on this subject. For example, Walter Chalmers Smith's hymn:

> Immortal, invisible, God only wise,
> In light inaccessible hid from our eyes,
> Most blessed, most glorious, the Ancient of Days,
> Almighty, victorious, Thy great name we praise.
> Unresting, unhasting, and silent as light,
> Nor wanting, nor wasting, Thou rulest in might . . . .[1]

"Silent as light." That's our God. We don't see Him; we don't hear Him, at least in a physical sense. Yet we're commanded to be wise and to understand what the will of the Lord is. But He doesn't speak.

Wouldn't it be easier if twice a week He would break the silence, visit us in our prayer closet or at our desk or in some part of our home and say, "This is our time together. I want to give you My will for next week." But if that happened, we'd be walking by sound and not by faith.

And so, since He is invisible and silent, and we can't read His lips, how do we get our messages from God?

LISTENING IN THE SILENCE

First of all, *we need to be sensitive and skilled* because God's will is unpredictable.

In Psalm 32 we find a dialogue between David and the Lord.

By the way, notice that this psalm is not only called "A Psalm of David," it is also called "A Maskil." A *maskil* is an instructive psalm. Also notice that right in the heart of the psalm the word *Selah* appears three times. *Selah* is a bracketed musical hint included by the psalmist, which calls for a pause. When you have a pause in music, you ponder what has just been played or sung as it lingers in the air, and then you anticipate what is coming next. In music, a pause can be very effective. In this case, there are three of them. And right after the third one come these words:

> I will instruct you and teach you in the way which you should go;
> I will counsel you with My eye upon you. (Psalm 32:8)

God is silent. So He does not say, "I will instruct you with My voice." He says, "I will instruct you and teach you and counsel you with My eye upon you." The movement of the eyes is a silent movement. So, like the lip reader, we must be very sensitive and skilled as we study our Lord and then respond to the inner promptings from the Spirit of God.

God's will is not only mysterious, it's also unpredictable. We've certainly established that, haven't we? Often it is not what we would have expected. Recently, a couple who are good friends of ours have been searching for God's will in the area of the husband's vocation. They had made a decision that seemed to be God's will, only to come up against a brick wall. For them to stay in the situation would be a compromise of this man's integrity. "So we're backing away from that," he told me. "For me to stay is to compromise my character. I won't do that." They are being very sensitive to what God is leading them to do, because it is obviously not what they had anticipated.

Second, *we need to be perceptive and patient* because God's plan is continually unfolding. What brought us to where we are right now is all part of His overall plan. But that plan is still in the process of unfolding in our lives, which means that taking us from where we are to His place for us in the future will involve change. And some of those changes are things we would never expect.

LEARNING FROM JEREMIAH THE PROPHET

Let's return to a biblical character we met earlier in this book. Jeremiah was a prophet used by God during some of the most difficult times in Israel's history—the last days of the kingdom of Judah.

> The words of Jeremiah, the son of Hilkiah, of the priests who were in Anathoth in the land of Benjamin, to whom the word of the LORD came in the days of Josiah, the son of Amon, king of Judah, in the thirteenth year of his reign. It came also in the days of Jehoiakim, the son of Josiah, king of Judah, until the end of the eleventh year of Zedekiah, the son of Josiah, king of Judah, until the exile of Jerusalem in the fifth month.
>
> Now the word of the LORD came to me saying, (Jeremiah 1:1–4)

"Now the word of the Lord came to me . . . ." Jeremiah has picked up his pen and begun writing. The pronoun "me" reveals it. I don't think Jeremiah knew he was writing Scripture. I don't think he had any idea that fifty-two of the chapters in the Bible would be entrusted to him. Jeremiah was just writing what the Lord had revealed to him, and God saw fit to guide his writing so that it became an inspired part of the canon of Scripture. So he records "The word of the Lord came to me saying . . ."

> "Before I formed you in the womb I knew you,
> And before you were born I consecrated you;
> I have appointed you a prophet to the nations." (Jeremiah 1:5)

God tells Jeremiah that He had set him apart as a prophet before he was even born. *Before* he was *formed* in the womb, God *knew* him. *Before* he was born, God *consecrated* him and *appointed* him a prophet to the nations.

God's predetermined plan is fixed. Before we were even conceived in our mothers' wombs, God's plans for us had been put into place.

In his book *Run with the Horses,* Eugene Peterson has some marvelous insights regarding this ancient scene. In the chapter titled "Before," he points out several splendid observations:

Before Jeremiah knew God, God knew Jeremiah: "Before I formed you in the womb I knew you." This turns everything we ever thought about God around. . . .

   We enter a world we didn't create. We grow into a life already provided for us. . . . If we are going to live appropriately, we must be aware that we are living in the middle of a story that was begun and will be concluded by another. And this other is God. . . .

   Jeremiah's life didn't start with Jeremiah. Jeremiah's salvation didn't start with Jeremiah. Jeremiah's truth didn't start with Jeremiah. He entered the world in which the essential parts of his existence were already ancient history. So do we. "I knew you." . . .

   The second item of background information provided on Jeremiah is this: "Before you were born, I consecrated you." *Consecrated* means "set apart for God's side." It means that the human is not a cogwheel, that a person is not the keyboard of a piano on which circumstances play hit-parade tunes. It means we are chosen out of the feckless stream of circumstantiality for something important that God is doing.

   What is God doing? He is saving; He is rescuing; He is blessing; He is providing; He is judging; He is healing; He is enlightening. And there is a spiritual war in process, an all-out moral battle. There is evil and cruelty, unhappiness and illness. There is superstition and ignorance, brutality and pain. But God is in a continuous and energetic battle against all of it. God is for life and against death. God is for love and against hate. God is for hope and against despair. God is for heaven and against hell. There is no neutral ground in the universe. Every square foot of space is contested.

   Jeremiah, before he was born, was enlisted on God's side in this war.

   God did a third thing to Jeremiah before Jeremiah did anything on his own: "I appointed you a prophet to the nations." The word "appointed" is, literally, "gave"—I "gave" you as a prophet to the nations. God gives. He's generous. He is lavishly generous. Before Jeremiah ever got it together he was given away.

That is God's way. He did it with his own Son, Jesus. "God so loved the world that He gave . . . ."

Some things we have a choice in, some we don't. In this we don't. It's the kind of world into which we were born. God created it. God sustains it. Giving is the style of the universe. Giving is woven into the fabric of existence. . . .

Jeremiah could have hung on to the dead-end street where he was born in Anathoth. He could have huddled in the security of his father's priesthood. He could have conformed to the dull habits of his culture. He didn't. He participated in the giving, throwing himself into his appointment.[2]

That is what I want for you! Wherever God's will may lead you, and whatever He may call you to do, wherever He requires you to live, whatever must be given up, and whatever must be taken on, DO IT! That is life at its best. The quest for life at its best means we run with the horses, we do His will, which is always the safest and most rewarding place to live—even though it is full of changing and risking and releasing. DO IT!

FIVE GUIDELINES FOR READING GOD'S LIPS

I've heard some Christians say that they pray only once and then they trust God. To pray more than once, they say, is to doubt. I question that. What about Paul, who prayed three times that the thorn in the flesh would be taken from him? Maybe he didn't pray beyond the third time, but he did pray three times, fervently. I don't find anywhere in Scripture that praying more than once is disobedience or doubt. We need to think reflectively, sensibly. God has given us a brain and His Spirit to work in harmony and in concert.

God wants us to understand what His will is. He isn't playing games with us; He isn't playing hide and seek with us. "No, no, no, wrong place, keep looking. You're getting warmer." He wants us to know His will. Though He remains "silent as light," He is engaged in directing our steps. He has created us to do His will. To help us do that, He has given us some guidelines.

To help me remember them, I've come up with an ultra-simple plan. I've used the first five letters of the alphabet: A-B-C-D-E. Frankly, I go through these five myself when I try to read God's mysterious lips.

A: An accepting frame of mind. I call this a "can-do" spirit.

To be in this frame of mind, we need to be relatively free of anxiety and stress. You say, "Well, I can remember two days in my adult life when that was true." And you're right. Most of us live pretty stressful lives. That's why we need an intimacy with the Almighty; we need times of solitude and silence. There's nothing mysterious about that. Some call it mystical. I call it wise.

I know a man who sets aside one day every month to do nothing but be alone, to be silent, and to think. For years, he successfully led an organization because of his commitment to that kind of discipline. On that day, he would eat a good breakfast and then fast at lunchtime. Then he invested the balance of that day alone thinking through, praying about various matters on his mind. Sometimes he took a Bible, sometimes he took a book, sometimes he took nothing. And he would go to different places—there was no sacred meeting place.

You may have a special spot where you like to go to be alone. For others, variety is important. One day it may be a walk on the beach. Another day it may be a trip into the mountains. It may be a long drive. It may be a walk around your neighborhood or just time spent on a park bench. It doesn't matter where, just so you have time to reflect where you're relatively free of stress.

What's important is that you have an accepting frame of mind— regardless. Regardless of where it may be or what it may include, you remain open. Teachable. Sensitive. Available.

Did Jeremiah have an accepting frame of mind? After God told him, "I formed you, and I consecrated you, and I appointed you," his answer was,

> "Alas, Lord GOD!
> Behold, I do not know how to speak,
> Because I am a youth." (Jeremiah 1:6)

Here is a prophet in the making. "I don't know how to speak." What did prophets do? They preached.

> But the LORD said to me, "Do not say, 'I am a youth,'
> Because everywhere I send you, you shall go,
> And all that I command you, you shall speak.
> Do not be afraid of them,
> For I am with you to deliver you," declares the LORD.
> Then the LORD stretched out His hand and touched my mouth,
> and the LORD said to me, "Behold, I have put My words in your
> mouth." (Jeremiah 1:7–9)

When we are listening in the silence, we need to be in an accepting frame of mind.

When I was in my freshman year of high school, I stuttered so badly I could hardly finish a sentence. One day our drama teacher, Dick Nieme, stopped me in the hallway at Milby High School and said, "I want you to be a part of our Thespian group." And I go, "Bl, bl, bl, bl, me?" He said, "Yeah, you."

I really thought he had the wrong kid. I thought he meant the guy next to me, who was a star basketball player. "No," he said, "you."

My first thought was, "Oh, I'm so inadequate. You have no idea how embarrassed I am in front of a group. You want me to stand there and st-st-stutter? I'll ruin the whole thing."

But only three years later, I had the lead in our senior play, I was on the debate team . . . and I loved it.

The late, great Dick Nieme, whose picture sits on my desk alongside my other mentors, saw what I couldn't imagine. He saw something within me before it was ever reality. All that happened to me is just an earthly, shadowy picture of the way God sees us.

An accepting frame of mind says, "Me? If you say so, I'm willing."

B: Biblical investigation. By now you know that God's will is never contrary to God's Word. You will never do God's will and then look back and find, "Oh, my goodness, this passage of Scripture condemns what I'm doing." It'll never happen. You're safe.

> O how I love Thy law!
> It is my meditation all the day.
> Thy commandments make me wiser than my enemies,
> For they are ever mine.
> I have more insight than all my teachers,
> For Thy testimonies are my meditation.
> I understand more than the aged,
> Because I have observed Thy precepts. . . .
> Thy word is a lamp to my feet,
> And a light to my path. (Psalm 119:97–100, 105)

God's Word makes you and me wiser than our enemies, gives us more insight than we had from our teachers, and provides us an understanding that's beyond the aged. That's an awfully good set of promises.

Now what does this entail? First of all, in searching God's Word for His will, find the subject that is closest to the area of need. Marriage, suffering, money, occupation, submission . . . there are hundreds of subjects. Get a concordance, which is an alphabetical listing of all the words in the Bible, and locate that word. If it's suffering, look up the word "suffering." There you will find a list of all the references in the Scriptures where the word is mentioned. Then begin your study on that subject.

Obviously, some of the things you might be concerned about

may not be mentioned in Scripture by that specific word, so look for synonyms. That's one way to do biblical investigation.

Second, stay alert to actual precepts and principles that you uncover. Remember the difference between "Speed Limit 35" and "Drive Carefully"? Pay attention in church or Bible study. This is not a time to drift. This is instruction time; this is a time to learn. Take notes. Jot down questions you want to think through.

Another part of biblical investigation is your time with the Lord. It can also be a part of your discussion with Christian friends. Instead of sitting over lunch and talking about the latest movie, discuss subjects of value. Remember, the lowest level of conversation is people. The next level is events. The highest level is truth and ideas. Call a friend for lunch and say, "While we eat, I'd really like to talk about . . ." By stating it, you set the agenda. You'll find you're eating less and thinking more. Pick your lunch partner carefully, though, because you want insight from this other person, and you also want the freedom to be vulnerable.

Finally, when it comes to biblical investigation, at the risk of being painfully elementary, I would suggest that you need a Bible that is a good, reliable translation of the Scriptures. In my estimation, the most accurate translation, although not the most readable, is the New American Standard Bible. The New International Version is also very good. The New Living Translation can give you a fresh slant on passages of Scripture, as does Eugene Peterson's easy-to-read, contemporary paraphrase, *The Message*.

Biblical investigation requires sound, sensible interpretation of the Scriptures. Study passages in context. Don't pick verse 7 and ignore verses 1 to 6. It's sort of like a diamond. Without a setting, a diamond is loose and can get lost. But when you put it in a setting, you can then enjoy the beauty of that gem. So it is with verses of Scripture.

God's Word answers most of our questions, but to find those answers takes time, patience, and effort. It's like a handbook or a manual of instruction for your computer software. You may have to dig to find the answers, but they are there. (When it comes to computers, of course, some of us may have to dig a long time!) You can read God's lips much more easily if you spend sufficient time in His Word.

C: The clarification and conviction from the Holy Spirit. This combination of God's Word and God's Spirit works within us like an inner compulsion. You're drawn, almost as if somebody has grabbed onto your clothing and is pulling you in a certain direction. . . . like an inner magnet, drawing you toward that goal.

When you're walking in the Spirit, and when you're thinking through the Sciprutures reflectively, when you're open to where God's leading, that magnet will start pulling on you, and you will sense a direction. It may not come quickly, by the way, but ultimately it will come. David says in Psalm 40:1, "I waited patiently for the LORD; and He inclined to me, and heard my cry." In *The Message,* Eugene Peterson paraphrases it this way: "I waited and waited and waited for Yahweh. And He inclined to me, and heard my cry."[3]

"I waited and waited and waited . . . and finally He did what He said He would do." Keep in mind, God doesn't operate by a twenty-four-hour clock. His timing is eternal. Furthermore, He knows His plan for us, even when we are so confused that we don't even know what questions to ask.

If you want verification of this, consider these significant thoughts from Romans 8:

For all who are being led by the Spirit of God, these are sons of God. For you have not received a spirit of slavery leading to fear again, but you have received a spirit of adoption as sons by which we cry out, "Abba! Father!" The Spirit Himself bears witness with our spirit that we are children of God, and if children, heirs also, heirs of God and fellow heirs with Christ, if indeed we suffer with Him in order that we may also be glorified with Him. . . . And in the same way the Spirit also helps our weakness; for we do not know how to pray as we should, but the Spirit Himself intercedes for us with groanings too deep for words; and He who searches the hearts knows what the mind of the Spirit is, because He intercedes for the saints according to the will of God. (Romans 8:14–17, 26–27)

Isn't that great? Paul admits, "I am in such an uncertain state that I don't even know how or what to ask, but God understands even my 'groanings.'"

Ever been there? Sometimes in prayer I've only been able to groan, literally. As remarkable as it may seem, somehow the Holy Spirit interprets my "groanings too deep for words" and places them before God's marvelous presence, clearly and correctly. The Spirit of God does that. Take comfort in that, you who want to word everything just so. You really don't have to spell our every detail of your concern. So stop trying!

I'm being totally honest here. There are occasions when I look up from my desk in the midst of some situation I can't see my way through and I simply say, "Help, Lord, help, help." I can't get anything else out of my mouth. "Help." And He does . . . He really does.

When we are willing to wait and let Him take charge of the problem, He will. The trouble comes when I jump up from my desk and say, "I know how to handle this. I'm just gonna take care of it right now." And invariably, I regret such actions prompted by the flesh.

Sometimes, of course, action is what God wants from us at that moment. But usually it's best to wait. As someone has said, "I never felt sorry for the things I did not say." I've rarely regretted times I waited. Often, the bigger the decision, the longer the wait.

D: Determine if peace is occurring. "And let the peace of Christ rule in your hearts, to which indeed you were called in one body; and be thankful. Let the word of Christ richly dwell within you, with all wisdom teaching and admonishing one another with psalms and hymns and spiritual songs, singing with thankfulness in your hearts to God" (Colossians 3:15–16). Let the peace of Christ call the shots. The word "rule" means "to serve as an arbiter," or to use a contemporary term, "to act as an umpire."

An umpire is the final voice in the game. He makes the crucial decisions, calls the fouls, and settles situations before they turn into conflicts. He keeps the game moving. That's the way it is with peace.

If you were to tell me that you were in the midst of a struggle and had just about come to a decision, I would say, "Do you have peace in all of this?" And if your answer was, "You know, I'm really unsettled. Actually, I don't have peace," then I would say, "If you don't have peace, you're still churning. If you're still churning, you're not there yet." Never move ahead into important decisions without peace!

For those of you who are married, let me add this: When it's decision time, your mate should have peace about the matter, too. Resist the urge to drag your husband or wife along against his or her wishes. I've seldom seen that turn out well. Some guys seem to take delight in doing that: "We're doing this whether she's ready or not. She's obviously not open to God." Wait a minute, she knows you better than anybody else on earth. She's part of the project, and she's your partner, which means you're one. In fact, you're so much one, Scripture teaches, if there are conflicts, your prayers will be hindered. "You husbands likewise, live with your wives in an understanding way, as with a weaker vessel, since she is a woman; and grant her honor as a fellow heir of the grace of life, so that your prayers may not be hindered" (1 Peter 3:7).

My dear friend Tom Kimber (whom I mentioned earlier) should never have gone to China if he'd had to pull Sue behind him, dragging her heels. And I know him well enough to say that he would not have done so. They went because they both had peace about the decision.

An extremely reliable theologian of yesteryear named Dr. Lightfoot writes, "Wherever there is a conflict of motives or impulses or reasons, the peace of Christ must step in and decide and prevail." What a great way to put it! When there is a conflict of motives or impulses or reasons, the peace of God must settle things down.

I do not try to talk people into decisions, and I don't talk them out of decisions. Sometimes there is a certain person we really want on our staff, whether at the church or at Insight for Living or at Dallas Seminary, and I feel that he or she is the right person for the job. But if they're unsure about it, I don't intensify the pressure. I've done that in the past, and invariably I've regretted it. If someone comes to me and says, "You know, I sense God is leading me elsewhere," I don't argue with that. Instead, I affirm and applaud the decision.

God doesn't give us His will for another person's life. He gives it to that individual. If a warning is appropriate, we may need to warn them. Or if we see peril in the decision (this could be the "wise counselor" role we talked about earlier), we may want to point that out. But ultimately the decision must be between them and God, who gives that sense of inner peace.

E: Expect struggles and surprises as you experience the results. "Consider it all joy, my brethren, when you encounter various trials, knowing that the testing of your faith produces endurance" (James 1:2–3). Sometimes we step into a situation that is clearly the will of God for us. We have reflected on it, we have gotten counsel from people we respect, and we have peace about it . . . and strangely, we're not in it two weeks before we realize, *This is a can of worms!* This is work! So even within the will of God, there are surprises and struggles. But we still have peace, knowing that we are the one who is supposed to deal with this can of worms. This is God's plan. This is where He wants to use us. But that doesn't mean there won't be mysteries—remember that!

SOME PRACTICAL ADVICE

I'd like to conclude this chapter with a couple of very practical suggestions. One has to do with the secret of knowing God's will, and the other has to do with success that follows it.

First, the secret of knowing God's will means we must get beyond all excuses and rationalizations. Remember Jeremiah's excuse? "'Alas, Lord GOD! Behold, I do not know how to speak, because I am a youth" (Jeremiah 1:6).

Did he think God didn't know that? God doesn't call you into a situation to be compared to someone else. You're called into it as an instrument. And in that role you are, in God's plan, invincible.

Second, the success that follows doing God's will rests with God, not you. This takes all the strain and the sweat out of the matter. Sometimes in the midst of a situation I'm so over my head that the only peace I have is in saying, "Hey, Lord, here I am again, totally inadequate. This was Your plan from the start."

That's when I go back to my biblical investigation of God's handbook and find things like God's response to Jeremiah's lame excuse:

But the LORD said to me, "Do not say, 'I am a youth,' Because everywhere I send you, you shall go,

"And all that I command you, you shall speak.

"Do not be afraid of them, For I am with you to deliver you," declares the LORD. Then the LORD stretched out His hand and touched my mouth, and the LORD said to me, "Behold, I have put My words in your mouth. . . .

"Now, gird up your loins, and arise, and speak to them all which I command you. Do not be dismayed before them, lest I dismay you before them.

"Now behold, I have made you today as a fortified city, and as a pillar of iron and as walls of bronze against the whole land, to the kings of Judah, to its princes, to its priests and to the people of the land. And they will fight against you, but they will not overcome you, for I am with you to deliver you," declares the LORD. (Jeremiah 1:7–9, 17–19)

I do not believe that we pull those verses out of context when we claim such things in doing God's will. I believe those verses have been preserved for our meditation and application, because I have seen God do exactly what He says here. I've seen Him take young, fresh-out-of-seminary pastors and place them in situations that call for wisdom and skill and gifts beyond their years, and I have seen them stand like a wall of bronze. I've seen women, because of death or divorce, forced to step into roles and situations they had never handled before. And I have seen them stand like a pillar of iron, surprising even themselves by their ability to handle the pressure . . . surprised that they are not overcome. When we're in the father's will, He steps up!

Please allow me one final return to Peterson's reflections on Jeremiah. Because he says it better than I could, I prefer to have you read his words.

His strength was not achieved by growing calluses over his highly sensitive spirit. Throughout his life Jeremiah experienced an astonishing range of emotions. His spirit registered, it seemed, everything. He was one of those finely tuned persons who pick up and respond to the slightest tremors around him. At the same time he was utterly impervious to assault and mockery, to persecution and opposition.

The thorough integration of strength and sensitivity, of firmness and feeling, is rare. We sometimes see sensitive people who are unstrung most of the time. They bleed profusely at the sight of blood. Their sensitivity incapacitates them for action in the rough-and-tumble cruelties of the world. In contrast others are rigid moralists, ramrod stiff with righteous rectitude. There is never any doubt about their dogmatically asserted position. But their principles are hammers that crack skulls and bruise flesh. The world makes a wide circuit around such persons. It is dangerous to be in their company for very long, for if they detect any mental weakness or moral wavering in us, we will be lucky to escape without at least a headache.

But not Jeremiah. Educated by the almond rod, his inward responsiveness to the personal, whether God or human, deepened and developed. Educated by the boiling pot, his outward capacity to deal with dehumanizing evil and to resist depersonalizing intimidation became invincible: "a fortified city, an iron pillar, bronze walls." Not bad for someone who started out as "only a youth."[4]

Let me encourage you not to rush in, as Jeremiah did, to rehearse before God your inadequacy. You think He doesn't know? *All of us are inadequate!* If we weren't, we wouldn't need God.

Our comfort comes in knowing that He does all things well—including His plan for our lives. His mercy rushes to our rescue. He is longsuffering and patient beyond our imagination, fully committed to using us, warts and all.

Part II

The Blessings of God's Will

Grieve not, because thou understandest not
life's mystery;
Behind the veil is concealed many a delight.

—Hafiz, *Divan*

Part II

The Magnificent Chesed of God

Entrust the past to God's mercy, the present to His love,
and the future to His providence.

—St. Augustine, *Confessions*

What value has compassion
that does not take its object in its arms?

—SAINT-EXUPÉRY, *The Wisdom of the Saints*

Chapter Seven

❧

The Magnificent Chesed of God

SEVERAL YEARS AGO, my sister Luci asked me a question that I'd never been asked before: "What is your favorite feeling?" Ever thought about that? My answer to her was, "I believe my favorite feeling is the feeling of accomplishment." (Sounds like a driven person's answer, doesn't it?) I like the feeling of getting something done. "Finished" is one of my favorite words.

When I asked her to answer the same question, she said, "My favorite feeling is relief."

I thought that was a great answer. In fact, better than mine! When I checked Webster's later, I found that the feeling of relief means "the removal or lightening of something oppressive, painful, or distressing."

When we are in physical pain, relief means that the pain subsides.

When we are emotionally distraught, relief calms us, gives us a sense of satisfaction.

When guilt assaults us in transgression and we seek God's forgiveness, the guilt that ate like a cancer inside us goes away as God brings relief.

When a relationship is strained, perhaps with someone we were once close to, we do not feel relief until we have worked through the painful process of making things right with that person.

When we are burdened by heavy financial debt, getting that paid off brings the sweet release of relief.

In chapter 5 we learned that the sovereign Most High God is ruler over our lives. So it's obvious that if we ever have the feeling of relief, God has given it to us. He's the author of relief. He is the one who grants us the peace, the satisfaction, the ease. In fact, I think relief is a wonderful synonym for mercy. Mercy is God's active compassion which He demonstrates to the miserable. When we are in a time of deep distress and God activates His compassion to bring about relief, we've experienced mercy.

Mercy. It isn't passive pity. It isn't simply understanding. It isn't mere sorrow. It is a divine action on our behalf through which He brings about a sense of relief. God, our compassionate and caring heavenly Father, is the author of relief. And when it comes to those mysterious, confusing times when doing His will results in the unexpected, there's nothing like mercy to make it bearable.

MERCY: OUR SOURCE OF RELIEF

The beautiful thing about mercy is that it is demonstrated to the offender as well as to the victim. When the offender realizes his or her wrong, God brings mercy. When the victim needs help to go on, God gives mercy.

And you were dead in your trespasses and sins, in which you formerly walked according to the course of this world, according to the prince of the power of the air, of the spirit that is now working in the sons of disobedience. Among them we too all formerly lived in the lusts of our flesh, indulging the desires of the flesh and of the mind, and were by nature children of wrath, even as the rest.

But God, being rich in mercy, because of His great love with which He loved us, even when we were dead in our transgressions, made us alive together with Christ (by grace you have been saved), and raised us up with Him, and seated us with Him in the heavenly places, in Christ Jesus, in order that in the ages to come He might show the surpassing riches of His grace in kindness toward us in Christ Jesus. (Ephesians 2:1–7)

"But God," the apostle writes, "being rich in mercy." The connecting link between a holy God and a sinful person is God's love, which activates His grace, which, in turn, sets in motion His mercy. They're like divine dominoes that bump up against one another. He loves us not because of something in ourselves but because of something in Himself. And in His love He demonstrates His grace, which brings forgiveness. And on top of that, grace prompts mercy . . . and there it is: *relief!*

To make it even more personal, look at Paul's own testimony in 1 Timothy 1:12–13. In Ephesians 2 he writes about everyone. In 1 Timothy 1 he writes about himself.

I thank Christ Jesus our Lord, who has strengthened me, because He considered me faithful, putting me into service; even though I was formerly a blasphemer and a persecutor and a violent aggressor. And yet I was shown mercy, because I acted ignorantly in unbelief.

Look closely at those three descriptions of Paul's former life. First, he says, "I was a blasphemer." The word means "an insulter." "I insulted God's people. I was angry at Christians. I accused them of crimes against God. I was a blasphemer."

Second, "I was a persecutor." He took every means open to him under Jewish law to hurt, to humiliate, even annihilate, Christians.

And then that terrible admission, "I was a violent aggressor." The Greek word suggests a kind of "arrogant sadism." It describes a person who is out to inflict pain and injury for the sheer joy of inflicting it. "I loved to make them squirm. I loved to watch them cry. I loved to see them removed from this earth!"

We don't usually think of Paul in these terms, but that's the way he describes himself before Christ. And lest you cluck your tongue at

Paul or wag your finger and say, "Shame, shame," realize that the same nature is inside of you. It may not work its way out in these kinds of actions, but it comes out in other ways. Most of us can remember acts of cruelty we've committed. What is true of the apostle is true of us. God showed Him mercy, and He does the same for us. (What a relief!)

Can you imagine what Paul's conscience must have been like when the Lord found him on the way to Damascus? Can you imagine the guilt? Can you imagine what he felt when his life passed in review while he was blind, before he saw God's plan for his life? Can you imagine how he felt? The enormity of the pain of his past? And to hear God say, "I want to use you, Saul, in My service"?

John Newton knew the same kind of anguish, which he revealed when he composed his own epitaph for his tombstone:

> John Newton, Clerk,
> once an Infidel and Libertine,
> a Servant of Slaves in Africa,
> was by the Mercy of our Lord and Saviour Jesus Christ,
> Preserved, Restored, Pardoned,
> and Appointed to Preach the Faith
> he had so long laboured to destroy.[1]

Some of you have been Christians so long you've forgotten what you were like before Christ. Could that explain why you're still so proud? Maybe that's why the Lord has to spend so much extra time getting your attention. You've forgotten how undeserving you are of His grace. You've forgotten His mercy.

I love the letter that an old Puritan, Thomas Goodwin, wrote to his son.

> When I was threatening to become cold in my ministry, and when I felt Sabbath morning coming and my heart not filled with amazement at the grace of God, or when I was making ready to dispense

the Lord's Supper, do you know what I used to do? I used to take a turn up and down among the sins of my past life, and I always came down again with a broken and a contrite heart, ready to preach, as it was preached in the beginning, the forgiveness of sins. I do not think I ever went up the pulpit stair that I did not stop for a moment at the foot of it and take a turn up and down among the sins of my past years. I do not think that I ever planned a sermon that I did not take a turn round my study table and look back at the sins of my youth and of all my life down to the present; and many a Sabbath morning, when my soul had been cold and dry, for the lack of prayer during the week, a turn up and down in my past life before I went into the pulpit always broke my hard heart and made me close with the gospel for my own soul before I began to preach.[2]

The wonderful thing about the writings of the apostle Paul is that he frequently returns to the sins of his past. He reminds me of what Great-heart says to Christian's children in Part II of *Pilgrim's Progress:* "You must know that Forgetful Green is the most dangerous place in all these parts."

Try hard not to forget what life was like before Christ and you will be a frequent visitor at the gate of mercy.

FIVE MISERIES RELIEVED

In the Old Testament the Hebrew term for "mercy" is *chesed.* It is a magnificent word, often translated "lovingkindness" or simply "kindness." When I trace *chesed* through the Old Testament Scriptures, I find at least five different miseries to which mercy brings relief. It's like that Visine commercial: "It takes the red out." Mercy mysteriously takes the red out of the anguish of your life.

The first anguish mercy relieves is the anguish of unfair treatment. For an example of this, we have only to look at Joseph, a great and godly man who was falsely accused.

Potiphar's wife comes at Joseph again and again. Each time he rejects her. Finally she corners him alone in her home, with the doors locked and the servants gone and the lights low. Seductively she whispers, "Lie with me." Joseph looks her in the eyes and refuses . . . then makes a mad dash for safety. She is so infuriated that she grabs at him, tears off a piece of his garment, and cries, "Rape!" The word gets to her husband, Potiphar, and Joseph winds up in jail, though he never laid a hand on the woman. The story is found in Genesis 39. Then, at the end of the account, *chesed* appears:

> But the LORD was with Joseph and extended kindness [*chesed*, mercy] to him, and gave him favor in the sight of the chief jailer. (Genesis 39:21)

Where did mercy appear? In a jail cell. In an Egyptian dungeon, the Lord visited Joseph and relieved him of the misery of suffering unfair consequences. God ministered to Joseph's heart and kept him from bitterness. God even "gave him favor in the sight of the chief jailer."

Chuck Colson has told me story after story about life behind bars, both from his own life experience and from the prisons in which he has ministered through the years. And mercy welled up within me all over again as he described each scene that transpired in those dark cells of loneliness and regret.

Here is Joseph in such a place, in great need of encouragement, and God demonstrates *chesed*. God gives him mercy.

You may not be in jail, but you may be going through a time of unjust criticism, even though you obeyed the Lord and followed His lead. You're in His will, but now you find yourself in need of His *chesed*. You may be suffering the backwash of unfair statements made against you. You need the kind of relief only God can give. It's the same kind the Lord extended to Joseph in that Egyptian cell.

Even when you are forgotten by those who should remember you, even when someone doesn't fulfill his promise to you, when you're left alone and you (alone) know your heart is just, God will give you His mercy. He'll bring you relief. He'll meet you in your loneliness.

The second anguish mercy relieves is the anguish of the grief of loss. The Book of Ruth provides a wonderful example of this.

Ruth actually begins with the story of Elimelech and Naomi and their two sons. Almost immediately we read that Naomi's husband dies, apparently at a relatively young age, and she is left to raise her two sons as a single parent. When they are grown, both boys marry Moabite women, Orpah and Ruth. About ten years later, both of Naomi's sons die, and suddenly the family consists of the three widows: a mother-in-law named Naomi and two daughters-in-law, Ruth and Orpah, grieving over the deaths of their loved ones.

Think of it. Naomi is probably still trying to get over the loss of her husband, and now she has to face the loss of her sons. And the daughters-in-law have lost their husbands. That's a lot of deaths in one family; the need for *chesed* is great. People need mercy when grief invades their lives. . . even when they are in the Father's will.

And Naomi said to her two daughters-in-law, "Go, return each of you to her mother's house. May the LORD deal kindly with you as you have dealt with the dead and with me. May the LORD grant that you may find rest, each in the house of her husband." Then she kissed them, and they lifted up their voices and wept. (Ruth 1:8–9)

Naomi says to them, "May the Lord give you mercy in your grieving. May He help you when the pain is so great and you don't know where to turn and when the lights go out at night you have no one near to put their arms around you."

It's easy to pass over this too quickly, especially if you haven't recently endured a time of grief. But at some time, all of us will. And when you do, remember that God has a special mercy for those who are left as widows and widowers, and for those who are left as grieving parents or grieving children.

It happened on April 20, 1999, in Littleton, Colorado. Heartbroken families were shocked to hear that their sons and daughters and one husband had been shot and killed. That morning they saw them off to school . . . that night they found themselves standing, grief-stricken, in a funeral home. If ever mercy was needed, it was then. Who could ever explain how such a tragic event could be included in God's permissive will? Mercy soothes such harsh times of confusion.

God's will may be for you to be a Naomi. You may be the one to put your arms around the grieving and to bring relief. In those circumstances, people need heartfelt compassion. They need your loving presence. So during times of grief God uses folks like us to extend His *chesed* as the grieving work through their sorrow.

The third anguish mercy relieves is the anguish of struggling with a handicap. To see a wonderful example of this, we only have to turn to the Book of 2 Samuel, chapter 9. It has become one of my favorite chapters in the Old Testament. It revolves around a man with a real tongue-twister of a name: Mephibosheth.

Mephibosheth was a grandson of King Saul. According to some ancient customs, when the king died and a new dynasty began to rule, all of the descendants of the old king were annihilated. So when Mephibosheth's nurse heard that both Saul and Jonathan, Mephibosheth's father, had been killed, she took matters into her own hands.

> Now Jonathan, Saul's son, had a son crippled in his feet. He was five years old when the report of Saul and Jonathan came from Jezreel, and his nurse took him up and fled. And it happened that in her hurry to flee, he fell and became lame. And his name was Mephibosheth. (2 Samuel 4:4)

Now, I don't believe that David would have allowed any harm to come to this child; after all, the lad was the son of David's dear friend Jonathan. However, not knowing this, for years this young man was hidden from the king. Crippled and forgotten, he lived a life of obscurity in a place called Lo-debar, which when translated means "no pastureland." It's a word picture of a place of barrenness.

Then one day, out of the blue, in the midst of all his pomp and prosperity, David remembers his dear friend Jonathan, possibly thinking about how much he still misses him—perhaps even still grieving over the loss of his friend.

> Then David said, "Is there yet anyone left of the house of Saul, that I may show him kindness for Jonathan's sake?" Now there was a servant of the house of Saul whose name was Ziba, and they called him to David; and the king said to him . . . "Is there not yet anyone of the house of Saul to whom I may show the kindness of God?" And Ziba said to the king, "There is still a son of Jonathan who is crippled in both feet." (2 Samuel 9:1–3)

The Scriptures don't tell us what was going through Ziba's mind, but perhaps he was thinking, "I'd better warn the king that Mephibosheth is crippled, because he may want to rethink his request." But if that was what he was thinking, he didn't know David or David's God, who has a special place in His heart for the handicapped.

The king never misses a beat. I love that. He never says, "Oh, really. How bad is the disability?" He doesn't say, "Is the boy on crutches? Can he walk at all?" No, instead, he quickly replies, "Where is he?"

> So the king said to him, "Where is he?" . . . Then King David sent and brought him from the house of Machir the son of Ammiel, from Lo-debar. And Mephibosheth, the son of Jonathan the son of Saul, came to David and fell on his face and prostrated himself. And David said, "Mephibosheth." And he said, "Here is your servant!" (2 Samuel 9:4–6)

Mephibosheth probably expected to be put to death. But David shows him mercy . . . God's magnificent *chesed*.

> And David said to him, "Do not fear, for I will surely show kindness [*chesed*—there's that wonderful word again] to you for the sake of your

father Jonathan, and will restore to you all the land of your grandfather Saul; and you shall eat at my table regularly." (2 Samuel 9:7)

In fact, David went above and beyond. He not only showed Mephibosheth mercy on behalf of his father (David's friend), but he restored to him all the land that had belonged to his grandfather Saul (David's enemy). And if that weren't enough, David made him part of his family. "There is always a place for you at my table," he said.

It's easy for us in an unguarded moment to treat those who are not whole physically or emotionally with pity or condescension, almost as though they are less than human. Mephibosheth even refers to himself as a "dead dog" (2 Samuel 9:8), reflecting the kind of self-pity or lack of self-esteem that sometimes accompanies one who is disabled. But David saw him differently:

> So Mephibosheth ate at David's table as one of the king's sons. . . . So Mephibosheth lived in Jerusalem, for he ate at the king's table regularly. Now he was lame in both feet. (2 Samuel 9:11, 13)

Isn't that *good!* Better still, isn't that mercy? I love the true story of the man who preached this passage and then he said as he concluded the sermon, "And the tablecloth covered his feet."

Every evening at supper there was stalwart Joab with all his military prowess and handsome Absalom and all the other members of David's household, and then as they waited they heard the crutches and they listened to the shuffling of feet until Mephibosheth sat down. And the tablecloth covered his feet.

God has a special mercy for those who are handicapped, . . . and let me add, also for those who minister to the handicapped. There's a special mercy that it takes, a special mercy that's needed.

Last year I was driving the freeway and I noticed a personalized license on the car ahead of me. It caught my eye because this plate read *"Chesed"*—that Hebrew word for mercy. And then I noticed, because we both took the same exit and I stopped right behind him at the stop sign, that on the dashboard of his car was a handicapped sign. It was as if the license plate was announcing: "I need mercy. Take it easy. *Chesed.*" There's a special mercy for those who struggle with handicaps of every kind.

The fourth anguish mercy relieves is the anguish of suffering. No one exemplifies this better than our old friend Job.

> I loathe my own life;
> I will give full vent to my complaint;
> I will speak in the bitterness of my soul.
> I will say to God, "Do not condemn me;
> Let me know why Thou dost contend with me.
> "Is it right for Thee indeed to oppress,
> To reject the labor of Thy hands,
> And to look favorably on the schemes of the wicked?
> "Hast Thou eyes of flesh?
> Or dost Thou see as a man sees?
> "Are Thy days as the days of a mortal,
> Or Thy years as man's years,
> That Thou shouldst seek for my guilt,
> And search after my sin? (Job 10:1–6)

Here's a man we've looked at before . . . a man in tremendous anguish, both physical and emotional. Imagine yourself in a hospital in the cancer ward where a person is dying in intense pain, and in the enormity of his physical pain, out come words like this. "Why do I have to live in this physical anguish? How much better had I never been born." That's how Job felt.

But then look at verse 12:

> 'Thou hast granted me life and lovingkindness *[chesed]*;
> And Thy care has preserved my spirit. (Job 10:12)

Even in the midst of Job's struggle with God's mysterious plan, out of his affliction there comes the magnificent presence of divine mercy—*chesed.*

If you have ever been close to someone who is enduring a lengthy time of suffering, or if you have been through such suffering yourself, you know that there are brief breaks in the pain when God's mercy comes over you like a soft-falling rain of relief that washes your sadness and discouragement away. How refreshing!

We are not talking about a handicap here; we are talking about a period of physical affliction. That is what Job is going through. And here he says in his anguish, "You have granted me life and You have given me mercy to continue, to endure."

I have a dear friend who stayed by his wife's side for almost a year as she was dying with ovarian cancer. He told me of such occasions, when the Lord gave merciful relief from pain. He said it was almost as if an angel of mercy hovered over their room.

When we're suffering the consequences of unfair treatment, there is mercy with God. When we're enduring the grief of loss, there is mercy. When we struggle with the limitations of a handicap, there is mercy. When we're hurting and in physical pain, there is mercy. All these earthly struggles that occur are no accidents. God is in the midst of them, working out His sovereign will. Yes, it's a mystery, which means we need special mercy to endure the anguish and misery of the pain.

The fifth anguish mercy relieves is the misery of guilt. And here again, we return to David, who offers us a clear glimpse into the tortured soul of a guilty man. Perhaps the most descriptive section in all of Scripture of the misery of secret sin and the relief of guilt confessed is found in two of David's psalms.

How blessed is he whose transgression is forgiven,
Whose sin is covered!
How blessed is the man to whom the LORD does not impute iniquity,
And in whose spirit there is no deceit!
When I kept silent about my sin, my body wasted away

Through my groaning all day long.
For day and night Thy hand was heavy upon me;
My vitality was drained away as with the fever heat of summer. *Selah.*
(Psalm 32:1–4)

When you deceive those around you, you're living a lie. And when the child of God tries to hide his sin, the guilt virtually eats him or her alive. But when you finally come to terms with your sin, and you make your confession, when you declare yourself guilty, God "surrounds you with His lovingkindness"—His magnificent *chesed.*

I acknowledged my sin to Thee,
And my iniquity I did not hide;
I said, "I will confess my transgressions to the LORD";
And Thou didst forgive the guilt of my sin. . . .
Many are the sorrows of the wicked;
But he who trusts in the LORD, lovingkindness *[chesed]* shall surround him.
(Psalm 32:5, 10)

We see this same pattern in Psalm 51. Same context. Same man. Same set of sins. In fact, look in your Bible and you'll see in the superscription, just below the title, that this is "A Psalm of David, when Nathan the prophet came to him, after he [David] had gone in to Bathsheba." So this is months after David had committed adultery and had Bathsheba's husband, Uriah, placed in the fiercest point of battle where he surely would be killed. David hugged his secret sins to himself until that day when Nathan courageously looked him in the eye and said, "You are the man!" And David's response, recorded in this psalm, is "Be gracious to me, O God, according to Your *chesed.*"

Be gracious to me, O God, according to Thy lovingkindness;
According to the greatness of Thy compassion blot out my transgressions. (Psalm 51:1)

"Lord, I'm at Your mercy," David cried. "Lord, I need Your mercy. I plead for Your mercy." And God granted it to him.

Do you remember the last part of David's great Psalm 23?

> Surely goodness and lovingkindness will follow me all the days of my life,
> And I will dwell in the house of the Lord forever. (Psalm 23:6)

God's goodness and lovingkindness—His *chesed*. His mercy.

Some quaint commentator once suggested that since this psalm is written from the viewpoint of a shepherd and his sheep, that last verse could represent God's sheep dogs named Goodness and Mercy.

Sheep of God, do you realize that these two faithful "dogs" watch over you and care for you? Their presence reminds us that relief has come. They nuzzle us back into the shadow of the Shepherd, who graciously welcomes us and forgives us.

TENDER MERCIES

When I am treated unfairly, God's mercy relieves my bitterness. That's what happens when *chesed* comes into my cell. I have been in a dungeon of unfair treatment. Bitterness becomes my enemy, but mercy relieves it. Mercy relieves my heart of bitterness, and I can endure whatever comes my way.

When I grieve over loss, God's *chesed* relieves my anger. Often that's the part of grief we don't want to admit—especially anger against the one who has left us and anger against God for taking our loved one. Mercy relieves our anger. Not instantly, but ultimately.

When I struggle with a handicap, God's *chesed* relieves my self-pity. That can be a major enemy for the handicapped—self-pity. When they finally come to terms with it in God's mercy, they are ready to do great things for God. But it takes mercy to get them over the hurdle of self-pity.

When I endure physical and/or emotional pain, *chesed* relieves my hopelessness. The great fear of those in long-lasting pain is hopelessness, the deep anguish that they cannot go on. That there'll never be a bright tomorrow. Relief seems gone forever.

When I deal with sinful actions, God's *chesed* relieves my guilt. Grace brings me forgiveness, but it doesn't do anything to my guilt. It takes mercy to relieve my guilt.

I love the lines from that old hymn, "Day by Day":

> Ev'ry day the Lord Himself is near me
> With a special mercy for each hour;
> All my cares He fain would bear, and cheer me,
> He whose name is Counsellor and Power.[3]

We often find ourselves in miserable situations . . . mysteriously, yet magnificently, mercy brings the relief that is so desperately needed.

One of my all-time favorite movies is *Tender Mercies*. It's the story of two opposites who marry. Mac is a man who has lost the battle with the bottle. The woman is a young widow whose husband was killed in Vietnam while she was pregnant with their first and only child, a little boy. After they marry, Mac battles with drink, but she never threatens him, never makes enormous demands. She quietly, graciously, and patiently, with tender mercy, trusts God to deal with her husband.

The story reaches its climax when Mac, in a fit of depression, goes out, buys a bottle, and takes a drive in his pickup. You're sure he's going on a binge. But he comes home late at night and finds his wife in bed, quoting verses of Scripture to encourage herself while he's gone. He walks in and says, "I bought a bottle, but I poured it out. I didn't drink anything." And at that point, his life turns the corner.

It is the simple story of a woman who loves God and loves her husband into loving God, and through tender mercies wins him to the Lord. He winds up in the waters of baptism, along with the little boy, his stepson. Tender mercies. Justice is tempered with mercy, and mercy is wrapped in tenderness.

When God commanded the Israelites to build the tabernacle, He had them construct a special piece of furniture for the holiest place of all. Not simply a holy place, but the holiest of all, the Holy of Holies, hidden safely behind the thick-veiled curtain where God's presence rested. This piece of furniture was a sacred box called an ark, in which the Israelites were to place the tablets of the Law and Aaron's rod that budded.

On this ark was a lid, and over this lid they placed two hand-carved golden angels called cherubim, one at each end, their strong solid gold wings reaching out toward each other. And the place over which the cherubim hovered was the most intimate place in the tabernacle because it was the lid over the box where the blood was poured century after century. Appropriately, this most-intimate part has come to be called "the mercy seat." When the blood was poured out onto the ark, God was satisfied. His anger abated as His mercy emerged.

Frances Schaeffer writes, "It was [Martin] Luther, when translating the Old Testament into German, who first used the term 'mercy seat.' It is a beautiful, poetic phrase—but it also accurately communicates what the lid on the ark really was, a place of mercy."[4] It wasn't simply a place of rigid, demanding Law; it became a place of tender, forgiving mercy.

As people of God, we must be people of mercy. Like the wife in the movie, we must lessen our demands and increase our compassion, just as our God so often does with us. His tender mercy so beautifully balances His sovereignty and His justice and His holiness.

What a mystery! God, who has every reason to judge us for our iniquities, graciously grants us His mercy. Mercy full of forgiveness. Mercy wrapped in love. The magnificent *chesed* of God, which we do not deserve . . . but from which we find great relief.

8

God's Mysterious Immutability

Behind the dim unknown
standeth God within the shadows
keeping watch above His own.

—James Russel Lowell, *The Present Crisis*

Only this I know,
that one celestial Father gives to all.
—MILTON, *Paradise Lost*

Chapter Eight

✧

God's Mysterious Immutability

No BOOK on the mysterious nature of God's will would be complete without several chapters on the mysterious nature of God Himself. We're in the midst of that as we continue to probe the Scriptures on this fascinating subject.

As we've observed again and again, it's impossible for us to fully understand the One whom we worship and adore, whose will we desire to obey. He is infinite. He is also our sovereign Lord—we've established that fact with clear scriptural evidence. And He is full of tender mercy, even though we sometimes question that, given our shortsighted view of life.

Furthermore, this One whose will often seems confusing and mysterious is faithful to the end . . . consistently and immutably the same. Strange as it may seem, our God stays faithful, constant, and ever-present in and over our lives, even when we cannot sense His presence, even when we question His plan . . . even when we have disobeyed Him, blown it royally and are suffering the consequences.

This is not only true, personally; it's true nationally. A nation can slide into a series of moral compromises that lead to tragic consequences. Those consequences can then escalate to such a degree that everything becomes chaotic. This happened to the ancient Jews. In fact, Hosea the prophet called it "reaping the whirlwind."

For they sow the wind,
And they reap the whirlwind. (Hosea 8:7a)

The prophet is describing his people, who had lost their way. Why had it happened? Moses had made it clear when they left Egypt and entered Canaan: "You're entering a culture that is idolatrous," he warned them. He told them, in effect, "It is a way of living that is opposed to your monotheistic way of life. Stay true. Stand firm. Be distinct. Don't compromise. No idols. No intermarriage. Remember Jehovah. Obey Him. Watch out for the signs of erosion!"

It wasn't long before the Hebrews forgot those warnings. Some kept the Canaanite idols. They may not have worshiped them at first. In fact, they probably just tossed them in a corner somewhere. But why not keep them; after all, they're just artful carvings. Then perhaps one of the children found an intriguing little figure and started to play with it. Later, he showed it to a neighbor who got interested, and before you know it, several people began to spend more time with the idol. And that led to further involvement . . . and more interest . . . until they "sowed the wind" and finally they "reaped a whirlwind."

In fact, if you take the time to make a study of Hosea 8, you'll see a series of things that led up to the whirlwind. "They transgressed My covenant and rebelled against my law" (v. 1). That's not simply Hebrew poetry; that's truth. They looked at God's law and they rearranged things. Can't you imagine their way of thinking? "This seems pretty strict for Canaan life. It made sense when we were in the desert, but we've got to look at things a lot more realistically now. A lot of what Moses said just isn't practical anymore. Our culture requres us to adjust here and tolerate there. I mean, these Canaanite women are not only attractive . . . they're lovely. What's the difference if our son falls in love with one of them? He's been raised right. He's not going to go off the deep end."

And so, in the process of sowing the wind, they "rejected the good" (v. 3). The implication? They embraced the bad. And when it came to deciding about their leaders, they slowly stopped listening to God or seeking His counsel, which led to a major compromise.

> They have set up kings, but not by Me;
> They have appointed princes, but I did not know it.
> With their silver and gold they have made idols for themselves,
> That they might be cut off. (Hosea 8:4)

Can you believe what you just read? These aren't pagan, idol-worshiping Canaanites. These are God's own people, the Hebrews! And it all started with one or two shrug-of-the-shoulders compromises. Something so simple led to so much sin, so much sorrow, so much suffering and, finally, an entire nation in exile. They sowed the wind, and they reaped the whirlwind.

Pay attention to the first few steps down the slope . . . because that's the culprit. And whoever continues downward sets in motion a cycle of complications. That's why God commands Hosea, "Put the trumpet to your lips!" (v. 1). Scream it out, son! Sound the alarm! Tell the people, "It isn't worth it. It isn't worth it!"

When Israel failed to trust God and refused to seek His will, they embraced the godless culture around them, which then drew them into a godless lifestyle. After a time, the godless lifestyle ruined them, as a people and as a nation. Eventually, the Assyrians invaded and conquered Israel, the Northern Kingdom, leading the Hebrews into captivity. At first, God's people lost their distinction . . . then they lost their faith . . . then they lost their freedom! They had reaped the whirlwind. Later, the same thing happened in Judah, when the Southern Kingdom fell into the hands of the Babylonians. Remember the psalmist's account?

> By the rivers of Babylon,
> There we sat down and wept,
> When we remembered Zion.
> Upon the willows in the midst of it

We hung our harps.
For there our captors demanded of us songs,
And our tormentors mirth, saying, "Sing us one of the songs of
Zion." (Psalm 137:1–3)

"Let's hear some of those songs of Zion. Let's hear you sing them now." And the psalmist sighs, "How can you sing the Lord's song in a foreign land?" They had lost everything.

They transgressed God's covenant. They rebelled against God's law. They rearranged God's words. The rejected God's will. They no longer listened to the Lord or sought His counsel.

Compromise always complicates our commitments. But never forget: God doesn't leave. Grieved and disappointed, He faithfully ushers in the consequences. God doesn't distance Himself even when He pours on the discipline. Why? Because He is immutable. Amazingly, consistently, and from our point of view, *mysteriously* faithful.

THE CYCLE OF COMPLICATIONS

One of the prophets who watched Judah's transition from compromise to captivity was Jeremiah. He prophesied for forty years, and he wept as he preached, all the while witnessing the erosion of apostasy. We have two of his books in the Old Testament. The first, of course, bears his name, which we have already referred to several times. But the second book, in my opinion, is even more eloquent. It is Jeremiah's journal of woe, called, appropriately, Lamentations.

We rarely use that word nowadays, but it's a great word. To lament is "to cry out with words of grief." It's like a wailing cry in the middle of the night. It represents deep sadness brought on by loss. And Jeremiah, as he stumbles through Jerusalem, once the stronghold of Zion, remembers and records all that they've lost.

Jeremiah remembers when they were a people of God. He remembers the warnings, and now, with a sigh, he records the failures. He reminds his readers that his people had set in motion a cycle of complications. By the way, that cycle is regularly repeated. It isn't limited to the ancients. Disobedience always brings a cycle of complications. God faithfully sets them in motion. I find at least three actions unfolding in that cycle. *First, when we compromise truth, we begin to be afflicted.*

> I am the man who has seen affliction
> Because of the rod of His wrath.
> He has driven me and made me walk
> In darkness and not in light. (Lamentations 3:1–2)

Jeremiah and his fellow Jews have certainly "seen affliction." That's the beginning of the cycle. When you do wrong, when you compromise with the truth, you begin to be afflicted, because God doesn't let His children play fast and loose in the traffic. He faithfully disciplines those He loves. He wants to bring us back. And so, in His mysterious will, He faithfully afflicts us with the rod of righteousness.

> Surely against me He has turned His hand
> Repeatedly all the day.
> He has caused my flesh and my skin to waste away,
> He has broken my bones.
> He has besieged and encompassed me with bitterness and hardship.
> In dark places He has made me dwell,
> Like those who have long been dead.
> He has walled me in so that I cannot go out;
> He has made my chain heavy.
> Even when I cry out and call for help,
> He shuts out my prayer.
> He has blocked my ways with hewn stone;
> He has made my paths crooked.
> He is to me like a bear lying in wait,

Like a lion in secret places.
He has turned aside my ways and torn me to pieces;
He has made me desolate. (Lamentations 3:3–11)

Does Jeremiah's lamentation resonate with you? Have you ever found yourself under that smarting rod of God? You may be there right now. You've walked away from His truth and are now suffering the consequences. Who hasn't been there? The pain is borderline unbearable. And you're supposed to hurt. He loves and cares for you too much to let you play with fire without getting burned.

Second, when we compromise truth, hope flees. Affliction turns to desolation. "He has made me desolate," weeps Jeremiah. "He has walled me in so that I cannot go out." That's desolation, isn't it? You can feel it in every phrase that follows:

I have become a laughingstock to all my people,
Their mocking song all the day.
He has filled me with bitterness,
He has made me drunk with wormwood.
And He has broken my teeth with gravel;
He has made me cower in the dust.
(Lamentations 3:14–16)

This is serious stuff. Jeremiah, God's prophet, had become a laughingstock to his own people. "Ha!" they said. "You're telling me that's the God we ought to follow? And you told us a few years ago that we ought to repent? And this is the treatment we get from Him? He's the one who brought all this on us. What a sick joke!"

"I'm humiliated, Lord," answers Jeremiah. "They're laughing at me." He records it all in his journal of lamentations.

And my soul has been rejected from peace;
I have forgotten happiness.
Surely my soul remembers
And is bowed down within me. (Lamentations 3:17, 20)

"My soul remembers and is sunk." That's the meaning of the Hebrew word here—*sunk.* "I am as low as I've ever been. I have forgotten happiness."

I talked to a man sometime ago who said, "I can't remember the last time I laughed, Chuck. I haven't even been able to smile for days." He described rather vividly the compromises that led to the lifestyle he had been living. He had gotten to the point where he was thinking of taking his own life. He had lost his joy; he had forgotten happiness. Then, in the faithful plan of God, I had the privilege of stepping into the man's life, and now he is not only alive, he's back in strong fellowship with God. Not because of anything I did, but because of the faithfulness of God. God was there all along, overseeing faithfully the consequences, waiting for the man to repent, acknowledge his wrongdoing, and humbly return to the joy he had left.

"For who can eat and who can have enjoyment without Him?" asks the wise Solomon (Ecclesiastes 2:25). Isn't that a great verse? Who can enjoy a wonderful meal, who can laugh at life and enjoy his God when he has distanced himself from Him? To have a joyful heart requires fellowship with the living God.

There's nothing worse than being responsible for our own affliction. It's bad enough to be a victim. It's doubly difficult when you've caused it. All of us who have "been there, done that" need no further reminder of those painful days.

F. B. Meyer, in one of his fine devotional books, *Christ in Isaiah,* wrote eloquently of the Hebrews' compromise and how they brought such suffering on themselves. Read the following slowly and with feeling:

> In the case of the chosen people, who for nearly seventy years had been strangers in a strange land, and had drunk the cup of bitterness to is dregs, there was thus added weight to their sorrow—the conviction of their captivity being the result of their own impenitence and transgression. This is the bitterest of all—to know that suffering need not have been; that it has resulted from indiscretion and inconsistency; that it is

the harvest of one's own sowing; that the vulture which feeds on the vitals is a nestling of one's own rearing. Ah me! this is pain! There is an inevitable Nemesis in life. The laws of the heart and home, of the soul and human life, cannot be violated with impunity. Sin may be forgiven; the fire of penalty may be changed into the fire of trial; the love of God may seem nearer and dearer than ever—and yet there is the awful pressure of pain; the trembling heart; the failing of eyes and pining of soul; the harp on the willows; the refusal of the lip to sing the Lord's song.[1]

Finally, when we compromise truth, God doesn't move. We do.

That's what happens when we deliberately walk away from the will and ways of God. Like the Israelites, if we sow the wind, we reap the whirlwind. The fact is, you see, God hasn't moved at all. He remains faithfully by our side, grieved over our condition. We're the ones who moved.

This reminds me of the couple who were driving home on their twenty-fifth wedding anniversary after a celebration at a fine restaurant. She was sitting over against the door on the passenger side. He was behind the wheel as she began to lament, "Oh, honey, remember when we were so close? I mean, I remember when we first got married. We sat so close that you could hardly shift the gears. And look at us now." To which he responded with a shrug, "Well, I never moved."

That's the way it is with our living God.

"Lord, I remember when we used to be close."

"I never moved."

"I remember when You and I were on speaking terms."

"I never moved. I'm still listening. I'm still here."

"I remember when I used to talk to You in very private moments and You meant something to me."

"I never moved! I never went anywhere when you chose to distance yourself from Me. You're still important to me."

Now, we've heard the bad news. It's time for the good news. And the good news is hope.

BECAUSE GOD IS FAITHFUL, HOPE RETURNS

We begin to see the hope in these hinge verses of Lamentations. They mark the turning point in Jeremiah's journal of woe.

> This I recall to my mind,
> Therefore I have hope.
> The LORD's lovingkindnesses indeed never cease,
> For His compassions never fail.
> They are new every morning;
> Great is Thy faithfulness.
> "The LORD is my portion," says my soul,
> "Therefore I have hope in Him."
> The LORD is good to those who wait for Him,
> To the person who seeks Him. (Lamentations 3:21–25)

"This I recall to my mind." I love that. Jeremiah is in the midst of sadness and affliction, remembering the bitterness of days gone by . . . lamenting over the "whirlwind" of current consequences. He is walking through the remains of the city he loves, kicking the debris and wondering how in the world this could have happened . . . and suddenly it dawns on him. "This I recall to my mind." The "this" points ahead. In my Bible I've circled "this" and then drawn a little arrow that goes right down through verse 32—which is the "this" that's coming; it's what he remembers. "This I recall to my mind, therefore I have hope."

When you are at the very bottom, hope will flee. And when hope leaves, a part of you shuts down. You can't even recall those verses that you learned as a child. You can't remember one line of one song. You can't remember one prayer you ever memorized, because your hope's gone. It was in the midst of that kind of bottoming out, that Jeremiah got hope.

What is that hope? It consists of three things, and I want you to write them down. In fact, I suggest you put them on a 3-x-5 card and prop that little card up where you can read it every morning. I'll tell you why in a minute.

Here are the three lines. They're right from the Scriptures:

First, The Lord's lovingkindnesses never cease. (If you like the word "mercies," you can put it in place of "lovingkindnesses." This is that same magnificent word, *chesed,* we discovered in the previous chapter.) "The Lord's mercies never cease." Let that seep into your busy mind. Some of you have been in such a hurry that not much has seeped in during the last fifteen or twenty days—not much, that is, from God. This glorious statement shouts from the heavens. It comes directly to you, personally delivered with your name on it. "My mercies never cease."

Remember the last lines of Psalm 23? God's two sheep dogs, Goodness and Mercy, follow us all the days of our life. They work to keep us in bounds, but sometimes we run. Yet even when we run, Mercy stays at our heels. Why? Because God is immutable. That's what this passage says. "The Lord's mercies never cease." Isn't that good? Aren't you glad He isn't fickle? Aren't you grateful that He doesn't turn away when you yell back at Him, or when you ignore His commands, or when you deliberately misread and misjudge His mysterious will? His mercies never cease.

Second, "The Lord's compassions never fail." (Here's the second line to write on your 3 x 5 card.) Interesting word, *compassion.* It means "sympathetic love, concern for the helpless." His compassions are unalterably the same. His heart keeps going out to the one who is running from Him.

This reminds me of the father of the prodigal son in Luke 15. The boy wanted all the inheritance that was coming to him, and as soon as he got it, he left home. Without an argument, the father let him go, just like our Father does. How long he was gone, we're never told. But when the son ran out of money, ran out of fun, ran out of food, and ran out of hope, he finally came to his senses. Everything he had looked for in all his "loose living" in "a distant country" could only be found back home. Somehow, when you're ankle deep in the filth of the pigsty, you get a different perspective than when you're fat and sassy at home, resenting the rules.

So when the prodigal "comes to his senses," he returns home. And his father, seeing him while he is still a great distance away, runs to him. Now, he does not angrily confront his son and say, "What have you been doing? Give me an account of your time. Where in the world is all the money? And look at the mess you've made of yourself . . . you stink! You're a disgrace to this family." No, no. None of that. Instead, he embraces his boy and repeatedly kisses him as he announces, "Kill the calf! We'll have a barbecue. We're gonna have a first-class family celebration! My son who was lost has been found. He ran away from me, but now he's back." This father is filled with compassion for his wayward son. He remained faithful, full of compassion.

So it is with our Father-God. When you come home, He says, "I forgive you . . . I missed you. I'm so glad you're back."

Finally, *the Lord's faithfulness never diminishes*. (There's the third line for your card.) Don't miss the progression here: The Lord's mercies never cease. The Lord's compassions never fail. The Lord's faithfulness never diminishes.

Even when you blow it? Yes, even when you blow it. Even when you make several stupid decisions? Even when you make several stupid decisions. Even when your marriage fails? Even when your marriage fails. Even when you knew better? Even when you knew better. His faithfulness never diminishes. See how Jeremiah expresses it? "Great is His faithfulness."

Now, when you've written those three lines on the card, set it by your bed. Read it every morning. Before you put your feet on the floor, look at that card, and read it aloud.

> The Lord's mercies never cease.
>
> The Lord's compassions never fail.
>
> The Lord's faithfulness never diminishes.

That defines God's immutability, which is a four-bit word for "He doesn't change." He has to remain faithful. Being immutable, He not only will not change in His faithfulness, He *cannot* change. He never cools off in His commitment to us. He never breaks a promise or loses enthusiasm. He stays near us when we are zealous for the truth, and He stays near us when we reject His counsel and deliberately disobey. He remains intimately involved in our lives whether we are giving Him praise in prayer or grieving Him by our actions. Whether we are running to Him or from Him, He remains faithful. His faithfulness is unconditional, unending, and unswerving. Nothing we do can diminish it, and nothing we stop doing can increase it. It remains great. His immutability never diminishes. Mysterious though such incredible constancy may seem, it's true.

Why is it when we lose all hope the enemy says, "Take your life"? Why is it that the enemy's favorite option for desperate, hopeless people is suicide? Why, in the dark night of the soul, does he prompt, "Put an end to it"?

I think the prophet provides part of the answer. Back in the Lamentations passage where we find our three promises of hope, there is another important line:

> The LORD's lovingkindnesses [mercies] indeed never cease,
> For His compassions never fail.
> They are new every morning;
> Great is Thy faithfulness; (Lamentations 3:22–23)

The Lord's mercies, compassions, and faithfulness are *new every morning.*

I don't know about your life, but I can tell you about mine. My hardest time is late in the evening. If I'm going to get low, if I'm going to get a little depressed, it will be when the sun goes down. If I'm going to have a battle that day, it will usually occur somewhere between sundown and bedtime. It will rarely be in the morning. There is something about the fresh dawn that brings back the hope that I'd lost sight of the night before. Are you like that?

There is a reason they call it "the dark night of the soul." In my forty-plus years of ministering to troubled souls, I've observed that very few people take their lives in the early hours of dawn. Most suicides I've had to deal with take place when the sun goes down—at night, in the darkness, when life just caves in and hope disappears.

Do you know what God's fresh, new morning message is to us? Whether the sun is shining brightly or whether it's pouring down rain? Whether the morning is bright or whether it's gray and overcast? His promise is the dawn itself. "Every morning," He says. Not every time you see the sun. The weather is insignificant. Every morning the Lord comes through with His encouraging message, "We're still on speaking terms, you know! I'm here. I haven't moved. Let's go together today." That's why I suggest you read those three lines every morning. It's a reminder from God that "we're still in business."

Trust God to remember you. He won't forget your name, He won't forget your circumstance, He certainly won't forget your prayers. He's not on the edge of heaven frantically trying to figure out who you are, or thinking, "What am I gonna do with her?" He's faithful to know exactly where you are. Trust Him, He remembers you. His immutability won't let Him forget.

I recall a wonderful promise that verifies this, written by the prophet Isaiah:

> But Zion said, "The LORD has forsaken me,
> the Lord has forgotten me."

"Can a mother forget the baby at her breast
and have no compassion on the child she has borne?
Though she may forget,
I will not forget you!
See, I have engraved you on the palms of my hands;
your walls are ever before me. (Isaiah 49:14–16, NIV)

Amazing! We are engraved on the palms of God's hands.

TRUST GOD TO REMEMBER YOU

How do we do that? Well, that's why God gave us the rest of this section of Jeremiah's journal.

The LORD is good to those who wait for Him,
To the person who seeks Him.
It is good that he waits silently
For the salvation of the LORD.
It is good for a man that he should bear
The yoke in his youth.
Let him sit alone and be silent
Since He has laid it on him.
Let him put his mouth in the dust,
Perhaps there is hope. (Lamentations 3:25–29)

If you want to trust Him to remember you, *stop running and start waiting!* "The Lord is good to those who wait for Him" (v. 25a). Stop running! Wait patiently.

Second, start seeking Him again. "The Lord is good to those who seek Him" (v. 25b). So, instead of ignoring Him, return to His open arms and start seeking Him again.

"Lord, I'm back. I know You've heard it before, and I know You remember me. I'm ashamed to tell You what I've been doing (as if

You didn't know), but it's good for me to rehearse it. Here's where I've been, here's what I've done; here are the things that brought shame to Your name and that hurt me as well as other people. I want to tell You today, as I come back to You and seek You diligently, that I come on the merits of my Savior, Christ. I haven't any merits of my own. I'm under His blood. I'm one of Your children, and I've been away from You far too long. I've acted stupidly. I've acted ignorantly. At times I've been both vile and vicious. But I'm back and I diligently seek You. I'm not going to ignore You any longer." Just dump the full load of your guilt on Him. He can handle it.

Then, stop talking and sit silently. "Sit alone and be silent since He has laid it on him" (v. 28). Wait patiently, seek diligently, sit silently. That means you need to stop talking. After you've poured out your heart, deliberately be quiet.

Spend a full day in quietness. Sundays are great days to do that. Set aside at least part of the afternoon to be completely quiet. Meditation is a lost art in this modern, hurry-up world. I suggest you revive it. Not by endlessly repeating some mantra to get into some other frame of mind. Not that. Simply and silently wait before your faithful God. Read a passage of Scripture, perhaps a psalm, and let it speak. Say nothing. Just sit silently. Let Him talk. Let Him reassure you that you are fully and completely forgiven and that your shame is gone. Feel His arms reach around you. Understand the cleansing that He's bringing. Feel again the freshness and relief of His presence.

Finally, submit willingly. "Let him put his mouth in the dust, perhaps there is hope" (v. 29). To me, this suggests no rationalizing, no excuses. Shove your mouth to the ground if that'll help. Stop trying to get around the heinousness and horror in your life. Face it. Submit willingly.

> Let him give his cheek to the smiter;
> Let him be filled with reproach.
> For the Lord will not reject forever,

For if He causes grief,
Then He will have compassion
According to His abundant lovingkindness. (Lamentations 3:30–32)

Like dominoes standing on end, those actions bump up against one another. It starts with love, leads to mercy, and then compassion; then grace washes over you as your immutable God gives you a fresh start. Stop fighting and submit to Him. It works. I know. I've been there . . . more times than I want to remember.

The beautiful part of this is that God will fulfill every one of those three lines. He'll show you that His mercies haven't ceased, His compassions haven't failed, and His faithfulness hasn't diminished.

David Redding speaks to this in a wonderful little book I've enjoyed for years, called *Jesus Makes Me Laugh*. He tells about starting a little flock of Shropshire sheep when he was a boy, which was how he got his dog. Read his words slowly. Picture the scene he portrays so vividly.

I had a beautiful ram. The poor man next door had a beautiful dog and a small flock of sheep he wanted to improve with my ram. He asked me if he could borrow the ram; in return he would let me have the choice of the litter from his prize dog.

That's how I got Teddy, a big, black Scottish shepherd. Teddy was my dog, and he would do anything for me. He waited for me to come home from school. He slept beside me, and when I whistled he ran to me even if he was eating. At night no one would get within a half mile without Teddy's permission. During those long summers in the fields I would only see the family at night, but Teddy was with me all the time. And so when I went away to war, I didn't know how to leave him. How do you explain to someone who loves you that you're leaving him and you won't be chasing woodchucks with him tomorrow like always.

So coming home that first time from the Navy [during World War II] was something I can scarcely describe. The last bus stop was fourteen miles from the farm. I got off there that night about 11:00 and walked the rest of the way home. It was two or three in the morning before I was within a half mile of the house. It was pitch dark, but I knew every step of the way. Suddenly Teddy heard me and began his warning barking. Then I whistled only once. The barking stopped. There was a yelp of recognition, and I knew that a big black form was hurtling toward me in the darkness. Almost immediately he was there in my arms.

What comes home to me now is the eloquence with which that unforgettable memory speaks to me of my God. If my dog, without any explanation, would love me and take me back after all that time, wouldn't my God? [2]

Yes, a thousand times yes. Why? Because He is immutable.

He's faithfully there. And hurtling through the darkness of your life will come this magnificent truth, which will wrap itself around you: God will keep His promise to forgive and welcome you home. His mercies are new every morning.

Remember that when the sun goes down tonight.

9

Can God's Will Make Us Holy?

Character cannot be developed in ease and quiet. Only
through experience of trial and suffering can the soul be
strengthened, vision cleared, ambition inspired,
and success achieved.

—*Helen Keller's Journal*

I believe that today in the west, and particularly in America, the new barbarians are all around us. We have bred them in our families and trained them in our classrooms. They inhabit our legislature, our courts, our film studios, and our churches. Most of them are attractive and pleasant; their ideas are persuasive and subtle . . . Today's barbarians are ladies and gentlemen.
—CHUCK COLSON, *Against the Night*

Chapter Nine

❦

Can God's Will Make Us Holy?

IT'S TIME TO DIG DEEPER into the mysterious will of God. In doing so, we must come to terms with our age-old, inescapable battle with sin. Can God's will result in our being holy?

We've just learned some things about the faithfulness of God from the journal of Jeremiah. Now, let's look into the writings of another great prophet of God, who was the most prolific and eloquent of all God's prophets. His name was Isaiah. Many consider him the most noble of them all. Certainly God spoke mightily through the man. What's more, God gave Isaiah eyes to see the invisible.

> In the year of King Uzziah's death, I saw the Lord sitting on a throne, lofty and exalted, with the train of His robe filling the temple. Seraphim stood above Him, each having six wings; with two he covered his face, and with two he covered his feet, and with two he flew. And one called out to another and said,
> "Holy, Holy, Holy, is the LORD of hosts,
> The whole earth is full of His glory." (Isaiah 6:1–3)

Isaiah sees and records something that appears nowhere else in the Bible: the seraphim, a body of worshiping angelic creatures, surrounding the Lord. Seraphs, mentioned only here in Isaiah 6:2 and 6:6, are heavenly beings that resemble flaming fire in their person. I say that because the Hebrew word *sarap* means "to burn." It's the same word that is used to describe the fiery serpents that bit the children of Israel in the days of Moses (see Numbers 21:4–9). So these are hovering angels, perhaps blazing like fire, or so full of zeal they become firelike in their worship. They surround the throne of God, ministering to Him in continual praise.

Isaiah does not tell us how many there were. Maybe there were hundreds, maybe dozens, maybe only a few, but "each had six wings" and stood above the Lord, swarming about His throne with their zealous and dramatic expressions of praise.

In this amazing scene, Isaiah is allowed to draw back the curtain of heaven and catch just a glimpse of the angelic creation and their activities. These are activities that go on incessantly in the highest heaven, which we never see—their adoration and praise of a holy God.

Not only could Isaiah see all this, he could hear the antiphonal voices in which they were worshiping, one calling out to another, back and forth: "Holy, Holy, Holy." Some have interpreted this to mean the Trinity: God the Father, God the Son, God the Spirit. I think, rather, it is a reference to the Lord's infinite holiness. When words are repeated in the Hebrew text, it is for emphasis, and rarely are words repeated three times. Here, this repetition conveys infinite exaltation. "Incredible holiness is due Your Name, O Lord God of Hosts. The earth is full of Your glory." Again and again, these mysterious seraphim called out such praises to one another.

In earthly terms, with the Israelites burning incense on the high places, worshiping like their pagan neighbors, the earth was not marked by evident glory. But from the seraphim's viewpoint in the throne room of God, the earth is full of God's glory. Don't forget that. Our newspapers will never report angelic praise. They tell nothing of the glory of God. They only tell what is occurring on the horizontal plane, and as you know, they focus mainly on the bad news. But the earth will one day be full of God's glory. Don't doubt it. Our current surroundings will ultimately be removed, and they will be replaced by that which evidences the glory of God. But for a moment, Isaiah was caught up in a scene that other people couldn't see:

> And the foundations of the thresholds trembled at the voice of him who called out, while the temple was filling with smoke. (Isaiah 6:4)

The temple foundations trembled at the overwhelming, thunderous praises of that angelic choir. The place was filled with smoke and with adoring, worshiping praise. And then, for the first time in the account, Isaiah records his own response.

Up until now he's only been an observer. I think if it had happened to you or me, the same would be true. We would be stunned. We would also be mute as we listen and gaze on this unique angelic scene. The first words out of Isaiah's mouth are,

> "Woe is me, for I am ruined!
> Because I am a man of unclean lips,
> And I live among a people of unclean lips;
> For my eyes have seen the King, the LORD of hosts."
> (Isaiah 6:5)

Isaiah's response to this scene of supreme, complete, infinite holiness is, "I am not even worthy to be in the presence of such a scene." *The Living Bible* paraphrases it this way: "My doom is sealed, for I am a foul-mouthed sinner, a member of a sinful, foul-mouthed race; and I have looked upon the King, the Lord of heaven's armies."

Isaiah sees the Lord in all of His glory, and then he suddenly views his own sinful self in contrast, and responds, in effect, "I am completely unworthy to be in His presence." God's pristine perfection was an eloquent and humiliating rebuke to the prophet. Gifted though he was, his sin-soaked humanity was painfully exposed as he found himself in the presence of pure holiness.

THE TRUTH ABOUT HOLINESS

Both the original Hebrew and Greek terms that are translated "holy" in the Scriptures convey the idea of "separateness" or "separation, a setting apart." In the Bible, when something is said to be "holy," that something is set apart for God, like our two words "dedicated" and "consecrated." The furniture in the tabernacle was "dedicated" furniture; the robes worn by the priests were "consecrated" robes. They were holy, in the sense of being set apart for the purpose, the work, and the glory of God. "Holiness" carries the concept to its maximum expression, indicating a total separation from all that is sinful, impure, and imperfect. Moral wholeness is encompassed within the word holiness, meaning that God is absolutely separate from any and all contamination.

To the surprise of many, it is the will of God for us to be holy, too. Remember Peter's words?

As obedient children, do not be conformed to the former lusts which were yours in your ignorance, but like the Holy One who called you, be holy yourselves also in all your behavior; because it is written, "YOU SHALL BE HOLY FOR I AM HOLY." (1 Peter 1:14–16)

But because the human race is contaminated by sin (thanks to Adam and Eve's fall in the Garden), we, during our earthly lives, cannot ever know complete holiness. At salvation, we are made holy before God by our position in Christ, but we can never know a complete sinless experience during our earthly existence. That's why Isaiah responds the way he does. By witnessing infinite holiness before his very eyes and hearing the deafening antiphonal angelic praises, he is reminded of the incredible contrast between his holy God and his own sinful self.

Why is it important for us who seek His will to know that our God is holy? First of all, *His holiness assures us that He is absolutely trustworthy.* Being holy, He will never take advantage of His children; He will never abuse us, He will never manipulate us, and He will never lead us astray. His will may seem mysterious, but it's never wrong. This holy Being who is sinless cannot do wrong. You and I can trust Him to do only what is right at all times.

Second, *His holiness guarantees that He has no deceitful agenda, no questionable motives.* When God leads you into His will, you never have to wonder: Will this backfire? Will this somehow work against me? His holy will is free of question.

Third, *His holiness represents a model of perfection.* Our God has not one flaw, hidden or observed, unwritten or recorded. Not even indirectly.

In an earlier chapter I mentioned that God will never tempt us to sin, not even indirectly. A person who sins will sometimes rationalize his actions by saying, "God set me up. I mean, after all, if it hadn't been for His plan, I wouldn't have a sinful nature. And if it hadn't been for the events—events that He's sovereignly in charge of, I might add—I wouldn't have been drawn into that whole mess in the first place . . . I wouldn't have been enticed." But mark this down: Because God is perfectly holy, He is never involved in our acts of sin, not even indirectly. It's not possible. Not only can He not be tempted, He also cannot tempt. That's right . . . *He cannot.* His holiness keeps that from happening.

So, what's the significance here? Well, consider this: What if holiness were limited to God and kept from us?

First, if we were not given holiness from God, we could not have fellowship with Him.

And this is the message we have heard from Him and announce to you, that God is light, and in Him there is no darkness at all. If we say that we have fellowship with Him and yet walk in the darkness, we lie and do not practice the truth; but if we walk in the light as He Himself is in the light, we have fellowship with one another, and the blood of Jesus His Son cleanses us from all sin. (1 John 1:5–7)

Light, here, is a symbol of purity. God is absolutely resplendent purity. As Isaiah observed, He is flawless in His holiness. "In Him is no darkness at all." Imagine, not one dark thought, not one dark motive, not one deceitful statement or act. In His nature and in His will there is no darkness at all.

And when we lay our sins before Him, He cleanses us. As His children, He gives us a purity that matches His own, and thus we can fellowship with Him. Imagine that. Sinful creatures though we are, when walking His will, basking in the light of His purity we have intimate communion with our God.

Second, if we were not given holiness by God, we would live our entire lives driven by evil motives, unable ever to be free of the darkness of sin. That's why Isaiah said in a sudden burst of spontaneous humiliation, "Woe is me! There's no hope. I can't connect, because of my condition and of what I see of Him. Woe is me!" And that would be true . . . except that God graciously transfers His holiness to us when we are walking in the light. Talk about grace!

Third, if we were not given holiness by God, we would not have the hope and assurance of seeing the Lord in heaven.

Pursue peace with all men, and the sanctification without which no one will see the Lord. (Hebrews 12:14)

The same word rendered "holy" elsewhere is here rendered "sanctification" here. If it were not for holiness being transferred to our account through the righteousness of our God, we would never see the Lord. That means we would never receive the promise of heaven.

I'll be honest with you here: That term "holiness" used to seem a little spooky to me. I thought I was alone in that concept until I came across a similar admission in John White's work, *The Fight,* in which he writes this:

Ever gone fishing in a polluted river and hauled out an old shoe, a tea kettle or a rusty can? I get a similar sort of catch if I cast as a bait the word "holiness" into the murky depths of my mind. To my dismay I come up with such associations as: thinness, hollow-eyed gauntness, beards, sandals, long robes, stone cells, no jokes, no sex, hair shirts, frequent cold baths, fasting, hours of prayer, wild rocky deserts, getting up at 4 A.M., clean fingernails, stained glass, self-humiliation.

The list is a strange one. Some items suggest you can only achieve holiness by a painful and rigorous process. Yet many teachers claim that your most intense efforts will be in vain since holiness is something God gives, not something you achieve. Again, my juxtaposition of items lends an air of frivolity to a subject which none of us dare take lightly. If the means by which men and women have sought holiness seem ridiculous, we should weep rather than laugh.[1]

Some people give the impression that we'll never be able to work hard enough to be holy enough. We'll never give up enough things to be holy. At the opposite extreme are those folks who see holiness as entirely passive. God distributes it. He dumps it on you. You enjoy it, take advantage of it, but you're just a passive part of the process.

Let me correct both of these extremes. First of all, we must be holy. Holiness always suggests, as I said earlier, separateness and difference. God, being holy, is different and separate from all other gods. And we, as His children, must be separate and different as well. We must live holy lives. We must live lives of ethical integrity and moral excellence. If that were impossible for us, God would never require it of us. But He does.

> For I am the LORD your God. Consecrate yourselves therefore, and be holy; for I am holy. And you shall not make yourselves unclean with any of the swarming things that swarm on the earth. For I am the LORD, who brought you up from the land of Egypt, to be your God; thus you shall be holy for I am holy. (Leviticus 11:44–45)

Those who walk in the light, obeying God's will, are actively engaged in a holy—different kind of—walk. Second, holiness is not passive. It isn't all up to God. We are active participants in the process. Holiness is part of the process of the will of God for us, His children.

> Who may ascend into the hill of the LORD?
> And who may stand in His holy place?
> He who has clean hands and a pure heart,
> Who has not lifted up his soul to falsehood,
> And has not sworn deceitfully.
> He shall receive a blessing from the LORD
> And righteousness from the God of his salvation. (Psalm 24:3–5)

Notice the involvement on the part of men and women as the psalmist described it: "Those who stand in God's holy place are the ones who have clean hands and a pure heart, those who do not lift up their soul in falsehood and do not swear deceitfully."

I think it is interesting that this Scripture mentions both our hands and our heart. Sometimes we think it is just enough to have clean hands. After all, people can see dirty hands. If we are unjust or unfair, people can see our unclean actions . . . our soiled behavior. That's obvious. So we "keep our hands clean," as the saying goes. But a deceitful heart—now, that's something else. We get good at deceit. We find ways to hide our true motives. A deceitful heart has no part in modeling the holiness of God. Remember Paul's strong injunction in his words to the Romans?

> Therefore do not let sin reign in your mortal body that you should obey its lusts, and do not go on presenting the members of your body to sin as instruments of unrighteousness; but present yourselves to God as those alive from the dead, and your members as instruments of righteousness to God. For sin shall not be master over you, for you are not under law, but under grace.
>
> What then? Shall we sin because we are not under law but under grace? May it never be! Do you not know that when you present yourselves to someone as slaves for obedience, you are slaves of the one whom you obey, either of sin resulting in death, or of obedience resulting in righteousness? But thanks be to God that though you were slaves of sin, you became obedient from the heart to that form

of teaching to which you were committed, and having been freed
from sin, you became slaves of righteousness. (Romans 6:12–18)

Shall we sin? "What a ghastly thought!" says J. B. Phillips in his
paraphrase. And yet many choose to live that way. "I've heard about
grace," they say. "I understand it's full of understanding and forgiveness, and I know that God always deals with me in grace, so I will
sin, knowing that He will respond to my actions with grace." May I
respond to that statement in all truthfulness? That is heresy. "May it
never be!"

Now, it's time to learn a major lesson in theology here. Without
Christ we are slaves to sin; without Christ, sin is our overlord, our
enslaving master. We can make all the New Year's resolutions we
wish, all the promises to ourselves, we can give all the assurances
imaginable to our accountability group, but unless we have God's
power within us that overcomes and conquers sin for us, we cannot
keep from serving it. That power is Christ's power, available to us
only after we have been converted.

When we come to the cross and give ourselves to the Savior alone
by faith alone . . . at that moment, the slavery to sin is canceled, and
we become enslaved to God. However, there still dwells within us
this tendency to do wrong. Because we're "bent" in that direction
within, so it keeps rearing its ugly head, keeps coming back, keeps
revisiting us. Even though we are right with God, we still must fight
the good fight—stay engaged in the battle against sin. Whoever
denies this is simply denying reality.

Let me explain how it works. God sees us in Christ when we
come as believing sinners at salvation, and He justifies us before
himself. (Justification is the sovereign act of God whereby He
declares righteous the believing sinner while we are still in a sinning
state.) Even though we still live our earthly lives in a sinning state,
God says, "On the basis of your faith in Christ, you are in Christ,
you belong to My family, I declare you righteous." At that epochal
moment God credits His righteousness to our spiritual account.

What a wonderful transfer! What a great relief of debt! Here's the great benefit: The hold that sin once had over you all your life before Christ is instantly released. You are no longer a slave to sin, unable to break its grip. Before, you had no choice. Now, you do. And the deep-down result is peace. Peace within. Peace with God.

> Therefore having been justified by faith, we have peace with God through our Lord Jesus Christ. (Romans 5:1)

And with peace comes holiness. He grants us not only forgiveness, not only righteousness, not only peace, but the capacity for personal holiness. Now the point Paul makes here is, "Since you have been declared "not guilty," what are you doing serving sin? It's no longer your master. Up until now, outside of Christ, you have been yielding yourselves as instruments of unrighteousness to sin. You couldn't help yourself. Do that no longer! Yield yourself to God. Walk in the light of His will. In doing so, you can take advantage of His gift of holiness."

Once again, this is where the issue of passivity must be addressed. Some say, "Well, when you do that, when you yield, you become totally passive. God does it all. You simply believe, and the rest is up to God." And I repeat, no! These folks who teach that may be well-meaning, but they are misled.

Look at these familiar verses and tell me to whom the commands are addressed? To God? No!

> I urge you therefore, brethren, by the mercies of God, to present your bodies a living and holy sacrifice, acceptable to God, which is your spiritual service of worship. And do not be conformed to this world, but be transformed by the renewing of your mind, that you may prove what the will of God is, that which is good and acceptable and perfect. (Romans 12:1–2)

The problem with a living sacrifice is that it keeps wanting to crawl off the altar. So when you crawl off the altar, my advice is simple: Get back on the altar. And you may have to do it every morning. Frankly, I do it most mornings of my life. I start my day with words like "Lord, today is Your day. Today is going to include temptation, and I know my tendency is to act in the flesh. I don't want to do that. I want to walk in the light . . . in Your will. I want to act in Your Spirit. I want to respond as You would have me respond. So I place myself on Your altar, and I ask You to assist me as I accept Your power to hold me in Your will. Help me to live like that moment by moment, all through this day."

It isn't all up to God. It is up to God to give us the strength. It is up to us to claim it and obey. When we do, His holy will becomes our delight. Remarkably, by walking in His will, we, sinful creatures though we are, experience what it means to be holy—set apart for God's glory. And the good news is this: When we let go, He takes charge and pours His power into us.

When I was younger, I worshiped in a church in East Houston. Inside that church, above the choir loft, was a large white sign with bold black letters that read, "Let go and let God." As a teenager I looked at those words every Sunday for several years. "Let go and let God." They sounded really great, and I'm sure whoever put them up there wanted them to convey that message to everybody.

Since then, I've learned the origin of the words on that sign—at least this is what I've been told. Back in the nineteenth century, a Christian college student took six postcards and wrote a large letter on each one of the cards: L-E-T G-O-D. "Let God." And he put them on the mantelpiece in a room in his dormitory at school. One evening a gust of wind blew through the room and the "D" blew away, leaving him with L-E-T G-O. "Let Go." The student took that as a message from God. He believed God had given him the secret of the Christian life: Only by letting go can you let God. I guess the end of the sentence would be "have His way" or "carry out His will in your life."[2] It's not a bad thought, but taken to an extreme, let me warn you, it could lead you into a rather passive mentality.

Nowhere in any of the wonderful biblical passages directing us to live a life of holiness do I see instructions to let go. Unless it's letting go of the former lusts (and that certainly is needed), or letting go of wayward thoughts so that we gird our minds for action. It isn't that God does it all and I do nothing. It's that God does His part, and then I do mine. God sends the signals, and as I read them, I respond in obedience . . . and that simple plan results in my experiencing His holy will.

My car has warning lights on the dashboard. Every once in a while when I am driving, one of them flashes bright red. When it does, I do not respond by pulling over and getting a little hammer out of the glove box and knocking out the light so that I can drive without being distracted. No, I stop and turn the engine off. In fact, I've had mechanics say, "Never just keep driving when your warning lights light up. Stop and find somebody to give you some help."

God has His own warning lights, and at times He flashes them, saying to us, "Stop, stop, don't, don't, don't, don't!" And if we're wise, we stop. We don't just let go and say, "Well, He's gonna have to take care of it." We take care of it. "We confess our sins and He is faithful and just to forgive us our sins." We use the necessary disciplines that keep our minds pure, and He does His part in honoring that obedience.

We don't passively yawn our way through life hoping by the grace of God that we'll somehow make it. We get actively involved in a life of holiness. In His strength, we supply self-control, we supply perseverance, and in our perseverance, godliness. (2 Peter 1:5–8).

We yield and place ourselves at God's disposal. Once we are yielded, He pours out the power, and we declare war on everything that is evil within and without. We live a life that is different— morally excellent, ethically beautiful. It's called a holy life. And He honors that. Because it's like He is. And according to Ephesians 5:1, we are to mimic God, living as He lives.

God has called us to be holy, so let's be holy. Take a really honest look at your walk. Are there any areas where old sins have begun to take control again? Those things you battled with for so long and finally got control of through the power of Christ? This would be a wonderful time to allow Him to bring fresh order out of longstanding chaos.

All of our Christian lives we have sung the old hymn "Take Time to Be Holy." Those words are true. It does take time to be holy. It certainly takes time to be mature. It takes time to cultivate a walk with the Lord that begins to flow naturally, because the enemy is so much more assertive and powerful than we . . . and so creative, so full of new ideas on how to derail us and demoralize us.

We need to lock onto that power that comes from God's throne. It's time we learned a never-to-be-forgotten lesson from old Isaiah the prophet. As he was willing to do, let's quickly and openly confess our human condition. Then, let's bow before our holy God's presence and invite Him to cleanse our thoughts, to correct our foul speech, to forgive us completely, and make us holy vessels who, like those winged seraphim, spend our days bringing glory to His holy name.

Can God's will make us holy? Absolutely.

10

Surprised by God

God is full of surprises. Mere superficial pressures never determine life's outcome . . . If you are intimately linked with the living God of the universe, you don't need to worry about what the crowd is doing—or even what the king is doing. The same God who created the world is able to carry you through and to work out every situation of your life, no matter how impossible it may seem.

—RAY STEDMAN, *Adventuring Through the Bible*

To be surprised, to wonder, is to begin to understand.
—JOSÉ ORTEGA Y GASSET, *The Revolt of the Masses*

Chapter Ten

❧

Surprised by God

It is one thing to sit in a comfortable place and read about being surprised by God. It is quite another to be in the midst of a situation that touches us personally and deeply because it came as a total surprise. But I have come to the settled that surprises are among God's favorite things. They are often the very best tests of how willing we are to obey Him.

Consider the day God surprised Abraham, who was well over one hundred years old at the time.

Now it came about after these things, that God tested Abraham, and said to him, "Abraham!" And he said, "Here I am." And He said, "Take now your son, your only son, whom you love, Isaac, and go to the land of Moriah; and offer him there as a burnt offering on one of the mountains of which I will tell you."

So Abraham rose early in the morning and saddled his donkey, and took two of his young men with him and Isaac his son; and he split wood for the burnt offering, and arose and went to the place of which God had told him. On the third day Abraham raised his eyes and saw the place from a distance. And Abraham said to his young men, "Stay here with the donkey, and I and the lad will go yonder; and we will worship and return to you."

And Abraham took the wood of the burnt offering and laid it on Isaac his son, and he took in his hand the fire and the knife. So the two of them walked on together. And Isaac spoke to Abraham his father and said, "My father!" And he said, "Here I am, my son." And he said, "Behold, the fire and the wood, but where is the lamb for the burnt offering?" And Abraham said, "God will provide for Himself the lamb for the burnt offering, my son." So the two of them walked on together. (Genesis 22:1–8)

Put yourself in Abraham's sandals. Try to imagine being that faithful. What kind of obedience did it take to bring Abraham to this point? What must have gone through his mind as he prepared to sacrifice his own son? It's unfathomable. I honestly cannot even imagine the emotions the old man had to work through.

Then they came to the place of which God had told him; and Abraham built the altar there, and arranged the wood, and bound his son Isaac, and laid him on the altar on top of the wood. And Abraham stretched out his hand, and took the knife to slay his son.

But the angel of the LORD called to him from heaven, and said, "Abraham, Abraham!" And he said, "Here I am." And he said, "Do not stretch out your hand against the lad, and do nothing to him; for now I know that you fear God, since you have not withheld your son, your only son, from Me."

Then Abraham raised his eyes and looked, and behold, behind him a ram caught in the thicket by his horns; and Abraham went and took the ram, and offered him up for a burnt offering in the place of his son.

And Abraham called the name of that place The LORD Will Provide, as it is said to this day, "In the mount of the LORD it will be provided." (Genesis 22:9–14)

Again, what kind of agony must Abraham have experienced as he bound his own son, placed him on an altar, and lifted the knife to kill him—all of this, if you can believe it, in obedience to the will of

God. And then. *Surprise!* God not only stopped Abraham from going any further, He also told him He now knew Abraham feared Him . . . and He provided a ram in a nearby thicket for the sacrifice. What a strange set of affairs! What an unusual process to take Abraham (and Isaac) through!

Have you ever been surprised by God? Years ago, C. S. Lewis wrote his testimony in a book called *Surprised by Joy,* where he told of his unusual conversion to Christ. But I'm not talking about the surprise of joy we experience when we come to Christ; I'm talking about being surprised, really stunned, with God's will for your life. If you are honest, I think you would have to say, "Who hasn't been? Who hasn't endured God's surprises?"

You lay yourself before Him. You pray. You ask for counsel. You seek His Word. You are willing to give up whatever you need to give up, and you move through the door, the door closes behind you, it is locked, and you know that God led you there, and then . . . boom! . . . your surroundings are a total surprise. You thought it would be one way, and it turned out to be another. Talk about unfathomable. Talk about unsearchable and infinite. Surprises—especially those that disappoint us—are all of the above.

CONSIDERING SOME GENERAL EXAMPLES

Several common examples come to mind. You get word that a dear friend, a middle-aged woman who has been healthy all of her life, is in the hospital. You go to visit her at County General. The illness is not considered life threatening, but she is running a high fever, and the doctor is taking her through several tests to pinpoint the cause. You leave the hospital, and on the way home you pray, "Lord, I love this person. She has lived a remarkable life of faith and has been a real example to me. I pray that You will give recovery and relief. Please release her from whatever is causing this fever." You drop off to sleep that night, peacefully confident that God has heard and will honor your request. You sleep well.

Morning comes early as the shrill ring of the phone wakes you. Another friend, who has been at the hospital through the night, tells you that your friend has died. You prayed, but she did not recover. And there is no way to explain why death happened to this healthy, godly, middle-aged friend who had many years of productive life ahead of her (from your perspective). You have been surprised by God.

Here's another. You're working at a job you love. Your diligence has been rewarded with promotions and raises. You're making a good living and your family is delighting in the benefits. You're enjoying where you live and you feel confident you're there to stay. Suddenly, you begin to have little squiggly feelings inside, a sense of uneasiness, restlessness. And you think, *Why? Everything is going so well.*

And then, out of the blue, you get a job offer. You didn't expect it, you didn't seek it, but you have to admit, it sounds appealing. There are new dimensions, new challenges to it. There's a sizable promotion involved, more money, but you would have to move to another state. The good news is, the climate is better there, and you've got long-time friends who live in that area.

You begin to seek guidance from the Word of God. You talk to people you admire whose walk with the Lord is more mature than yours. You pray. You wait. Ultimately, you think, "Why sure, this is the way God does it—He's providing a whole new and exciting opportunity. Why Not?" You are at peace about the decision. So you resign, and move. It isn't three months before you realize, *I don't fit here.* This isn't what you expected. You try to make it work. You think, *If I just work harder and longer, and if I just give it more time, then it'll turn around.* But it doesn't. Things only get worse. And within a few months, you've lost that job. His unsearchable, unfathomable, infinite plan that you can't explain, results in your being surprised by God.

In the mystery of God's will we sometimes come to a place where we cannot explain why things turned out as they did; yet, amazingly, we are still right in the middle of His will. It's not that you or I created a problem; it's that God is in the process of surprising His people on a regular basis. As we've illustrated throughout this book, the Scriptures are full of stories like this.

Now before we go any further, let me answer the skeptic who is thinking, *Well, maybe God isn't really involved in all these 'surprises' at all. This is just life happening, running its random course. Maybe God just operates from a distance. He's a big picture God. He's sort of involved in the nations and the international scene and wars and those kind of things, but when it comes to daily living, He's not really that connected.*

Oh, no. The Bible includes numerous statements that refute that idea. Here are only three of them:

> For He looks to the ends of the earth,
> And sees everything under the heavens. (Job 28:24)

> Thou dost scrutinize my path and my lying down,
> And art intimately acquainted with all my ways. (Psalm 139:3)

> For the ways of a man are before the eyes of the LORD,
> And He watches all his paths. (Proverbs 5:21)

Doesn't sound to me like a distant Deity. He is exacting in His knowledge. As we have already learned, He is sovereign over all the events of our lives. Not one detail escapes His attention. The very hairs of our head are numbered. He knows everything about us. We are an open book before Him. Furthermore, He is immutably faithful. And yet He deliberately surprises us with difficult assignments, premature or unexpected deaths, lost jobs, and disappointing circumstances along the journey, even while we're in the nucleus of His will. Let's face it, it's a mystery.

RETURNING TO A SPECIFIC EXAMPLE

Let's go back and dig a little deeper into Abraham's test, recorded in Genesis 22. There we see God speaking clearly and forthrightly. He does not stutter, nor hesitate in His command: "Take your son, your only son, Isaac, whom you love . . . ."

Ishmael and Hagar have been sent away by this point in Abraham's life. But lest Abraham be tempted to search for Ishmael and offer him, God states specifically, "I want Isaac on that altar. Offer him up as a burnt offering." The Hebrew word is *olah*, which means "a whole burnt offering." If it were used of an animal, it would mean from hoof to head, all of it. "I want Isaac on an altar, consumed in fire, and the aroma coming up to Me will be an act of worship on your part, Abraham."

You know what's remarkable to me? We don't read of an argument or even a moment's hesitation on Abraham's part. And in case you think Isaac is just a little boy, a toddler, note that when they get to the mountain, he carries the wood for the fire. So Isaac is probably in his mid- to late-teen years, at least.

And on the way, there is this dialogue that touches me every time I read it. Isaac says, "Father!" And Abraham answers, "Yes, son." Isaac continues, "We've got the fire and the wood, but where's the lamb? Where's the sacrifice?" Isaac has seen his father offer sacrifices before. He's knows the drill. "Dad, . . . what do you plan to use for a sacrifice?"

Abraham's answer is nothing short of magnificent: "God will provide, my son . . . God will provide the sacrifice."

God is not like us. We have established that at length in the previous chapters. His ways are higher than our ways, and His will is different than our wills. God has a plan that's deeper than anything you and I can envision, let alone figure out.

This is a checkpoint of Abraham's faith. "Is your fear of Me greater than your love for your boy? Is your confidence in Me stronger than your affection for your very own son?"

And Abraham passes the test. Totally and stoically obedient, the man builds the altar, arranges the wood, and binds his son. On Isaac's part there's no wrestling to get free. Isaac now gets the picture. Abraham places him on the altar on top of the wood. And I'm convinced he would have brought the knife right down into his son's chest had God not intervened with another surprise.

But the Lord calls out, "Abraham! Abraham!"

And he says, "Here I am."

And the Lord says, "Don't strike that blow. Don't sacrifice your son. You have feared and obeyed Me above all—even your precious child."

You talk about being surprised. This is a wonderful surprise. This is what I call a domestic crisis surprise. Words fail to convey how precious children are to their parents. Yet in the plan of God, who plants that parental love deep in our hearts, He also, in one way or another, has ways that help us release them to Him one by one. It is one thing to love our children and care for them, watch over them and provide for them; it's another thing to place them on a level of adoration above our adoration of God. It is one thing to be grateful for them, to nurture them, and to train them; it is another thing to make idols out of them.

Someone said to me recently that God provides us with things, it seems, only for the purpose that we might learn to release them back to Him. He wants us to hold all things loosely. To release all things to Him.

Is the Lord going to use you in a great way? Quite probably. Is He going to prepare you as you expect? Probably not. And if you're not careful, you will look at the trials, the tests, the sudden interruptions, the disappointments, the sadness, the lost jobs, the failed opportunities, the broken moments, and you will think, *He's through with me. He's finished with me,* when in fact He is equipping you.

"It's doubtful God can use anyone greatly till he's hurt him deeply," said A. W. Tozer.[1]

Why do I dwell on this so deliberately? Why have I returned to it throughout this book? Because I'm convinced that these experiences are not the exception; they are the rule. Our idea of the will of God is that He leads as we would lead and plans as we would plan. But that's not the case. His will is not like that at all. In fact, here are four simple principles we need to keep in mind regarding God's leading.

First: God's preferred method is surprise. So expect surprises. I repeat, surprises are the rule, not the exception.

Second: His surprises require flexibility and adaptability. When you get in a situation that you didn't expect, you have to adapt; you are forced to adjust. God hasn't made a mistake. You haven't made a mistake. You're just going through the process of internal development that is all part of God's arrangement of events, painful though that may be.

In our home, Cynthia calls these changes "Plan B" arrangements. "Well, we go to Plan B today," she'll often say. We expected Plan A; it seemed so clear. Then, out of the blue comes a surprise, and we're left with another whole series of plans. Plan B kicks in as we flex to our Father's surprising will.

Third: Behind God's surprises are purposes we are not aware of. Evaluate them. Remind yourself that this is no mistake. This is no accident. God has deliberately planned this. Rather than feeling sorry for yourself, pray, "Lord, give me some insight here. Help me to understand why my job isn't what I thought it would be. Help me learn what I can learn through this loss, through this whole rearrangement of events. Why did You disrupt my plans and move me so obviously from there to here? Why is it that after I prayed Your answer was no? What is it You want me to learn in this process? Rather than becoming embittered, angered, and disillusioned, rather than calling the whole thing "a mistake," ask, "What can I learn from this?"

Fourth: When God surprises us, He supplies sufficient grace to handle the unexpected. As we lean on Him, He supplies what we need to endure whatever His will encompasses for us.

When I spoke of this in a sermon recently, a member of our congregation, who is going through a difficult test with two of his children, handed me this note: "Thanks, Chuck. Grace is sufficient, but sometimes the process is scary." And it is.

God's surprises can be very scary, very unsettling. They can push you to the absolute limit. But you know what you're learning to do in this process of dealing with God's surprises? You're learning to think theologically. . . . to view life from a vertical perspective. By doing so, you can release your child. You can even accept mistreatment without becoming bitter. You can handle delayed gratification and learn patience. The list goes on and on.

The sovereign God of surprises still reigns supreme. How grateful I am for that. And it could be the biggest surprise of my life, or your life, is just ahead. Or perhaps you're right in the midst of one of those surprises.

It's possible that God's surprise is intended to help you to see for the first time in your whole life your great need for Him. Maybe you have gone your own way throughout your years. And now, through a chain of events too complicated to describe, you are realizing, "There's never been a time in my life when I've really surrendered anything to this invisible God you're talking about."

Wherever you are in this journey called life, wherever you may be employed, wherever you may be in your domestic situation, wherever you may be in your age, your health, or your lifestyle, God may be preparing you for a great surprise in order to find you faithful. Rather than running from Him, let me suggest the opposite: Run *toward* Him. And rather than looking for someone to blame for the pain that you're now enduring or the change that's on the horizon, look heavenward and realize that this arrangement is sovereignly put together for your good and for His glory.

It's a wonderful thing when we learn how to turn His surprises into opportunities to surrender whatever we've been clinging to these many years. But I need to warn you: It is never easy.

For Abraham, it was Isaac. What is it for you?

11

Closed Doors, Open Doors

Ah, what a dusty answer gets the soul when hot for certainties in this our life!

—George Meredith, *Modern Love*

When the oak tree is felled, the whole forest echoes with it; but a hundred acorns are planted silently by some unnoticed breeze.
—THOMAS CARLYLE, *On History*

Chapter Eleven

❦

Closed Doors, Open Doors

Y OU AND I have traveled quite a ways together through these pages. We've been reminded of some things we'd forgotten, and we've learned some things we didn't know before. I can't speak for you, but I can say it's been a helpful journey for me. I needed this trip, having spent these last five-plus years where I never thought I'd be. But I had no other choice. God slammed all the other doors shut.

A slammed door is a harsh sound. It's not an easy sound to listen to. And it's an even harder thing to experience, especially if you have genuinely sought God's will.

You've prayed, you've sought the counsel of people you admire, you've studied sections of His Word that might very well lead you into the way you ought to go, you've spent time alone, weighing the pros and cons, your heart is willing, your spirit is ready, your soul is soaring. And about the time you get near it, bang! . . . the door slams shut.

That can be very disillusioning. Painfully disappointing.

I'm not saying it closed because you were living in sin or because your heart was turned against what God wanted or because you were selfish in some way. It just closed. Nobody can explain why. And you sort of reel and step back. You talk to the Lord and it's as though the heavens are brass. The door has closed. Period. End of story. Or is it?

185

You cultivate a relationship with this fine individual, and you go together for months, sometimes more than a year, and you fall deeply in love with that person. And just before you get to the subject of marriage, bang! . . . the romance cools and the relationship ends. Closed door.

You've got your heart set on a particular school. You've got the grades, you've got a good resumé, and you've got the background to do the work academically. But they can take just so many, and when the final cut comes, bang! . . . you're not chosen. You can almost hear the door slammed shut. No explanation, no reason. You're disillusioned.

I want to tell you that Cynthia and I, in almost forty-five years of marriage, have encountered a few closed doors that to this day we still cannot explain. With all our hearts we sought to do what we believed to be the will of God. We asked for guidance, we laid ourselves before Him, we held nothing tightly, willing to give up whatever needed to be given up to make it happen. Bang! Closed door.

By now, we hardly need the reminder that the Christian life is not a cloud-nine utopia. And if you still think it is, after all we've dealt with in these chapters, then I am going to burst that balloon once and for all. Because that's not only a terribly unrealistic view, thinking that Christ helps you live happily ever after; it's downright unbiblical! Once we're in heaven, sure, that's a different story. But until then, there are not many days you could write in your journal as fantastic, unbelievable, incredible, or remarkable. Most of life is learning and growing, falling and getting back up, forgiving and forgetting, accepting and going on.

Dr. Bruce Waltke, one of my mentors in the Hebrew language at seminary, used to say, "The longer I live and the closer I walk with Christ, the more I believe He does not take the time to explain why. So we trust Him through our lives without expecting the 'why?' to be answered."

I find a similar kind of comfort in the third chapter of Revelation. This chapter not only has something to say about who's in charge of closed doors, it also puts the responsibility where it belongs: squarely on the Lord.

Earlier, I mentioned the sovereign Potter doing with the clay as He pleases. I've watched a few potters at work. And it's a funny thing. I have seen them suddenly mash the clay down and start over again. Each time they do this, the clay comes out looking entirely different. And with gifted potters, they can start over and over— each time it's better and better.

He is the Potter, we are the clay. He is the one who gives the commands; we are the ones who obey. He never has to explain Himself; He never has to ask permission. Nor does He predict ahead of time that we're just about to encounter a closed door. He is shaping us into the image of His Son, regardless of the pain and heartache that may require. Those lessons are learned a little easier when we remember that we are not in charge, He is. That very thought is underscored in the last book of the Bible.

WHO HOLDS THE KEY?

In Revelation 3, as John writes under the direction of the Holy Spirit, the Lord Jesus Christ has the floor and is telling John to write to the messenger of the church at Philadelphia.

And to the angel of the church in Philadelphia write:
He who is holy, who is true, who has the key of David, who opens and no one will shut, and who shuts and no one opens, says this: "I know your deeds. Behold, I have put before you an open door which no one can shut, because you have a little power, and have kept My word, and have not denied My name." (Revelation 3:7–8)

Here our Lord defines Himself as the one "who is holy," . . . that is, sinless, the one "who is true." And by that He means He hates evil, and He does not counsel in error or engage in erroneous activities. He is "holy," He is "true," and He "has the key of David," which is symbolic for authority.

Someone who has the key to the safe has the authority to open the safe. You have a key to your home. That gives you the authority to go into the home. Whoever doesn't have the key has no right to invade a home.

Since Jesus "has the key of David," clearly He has the authority. And look at the description of that authority: He describes himself as the one "who opens and no one will shut, who shuts and no one opens." He alone has the right to open a door of opportunity and escort us through it. And we enjoy the benefits as well as endure the tests. As He walks with us, we persevere through the doors He opens. He also has the right to slam doors without explanation. And more often than not, when a door of opportunity is shut, it is to lead us through a better door with greater opportunities. Closed doors . . . open doors: Either is God's prerogative.

You don't live very long in the Christian life before you realize that both happen regularly. As profoundly as we may pray and as consistently as we may make ourselves available to do the Lord's will, there are times that His answer is no. That's right . . . no. Closed door.

Now it's our tendency, being only human, to use a little force when we encounter a closed door. After all, we've worked pretty hard for this plan. I mean, we gave up what we had over there and we moved over here, and we're not going to take a closed door sitting down. So we get out the crowbar of ingenuity, or we use some dynamite of carnality, and we start working on the door, because we're gonna get that door open.

Stop . . . stop. Take it from one who's done that too many times. Anytime you force a door, thinking you'll get your way, ultimately you will regret it. Leave it closed, back away, accept it. In acceptance lies peace.

A CLASSIC EXAMPLE

In Acts 16 we find an example of how this occurred in the lives of some of God's true servants. Here we find two missionaries on their way across Turkey, which is called Asia in this biblical account. They travel from the southeastern part of the country to the westernmost region, and it is remarkable what they encounter. Understand, Paul and Silas have great hearts. They desire to make Christ known; they have no selfish motives; they are not in this for themselves. Paul has already had one successful missionary journey. Oh, it had its trials, but what a success it was! And the church at Antioch that sent them out before has now sent them out again. This time, though, rather than crossing the Aegean Sea, they are going by land.

So they come "to Derbe and to Lystra," where they were before, and while in Lystra, the Lord leads them to the young man named Timothy (Acts 16:1). So Paul and Silas link arms with young Timothy and he begins to travel with them. And "the churches were being strengthened in the faith, and were increasing in number daily" (Acts 16:5).

This is remarkable. They are in a pagan region. This is idolatrous country. Yet all across the area, people are coming to Christ, churches are being founded. *Why,* they must have thought, *we are in for the time of our lives.* So they leave the familiar area and move on toward the Phrygian/Galatian region with high hopes. Read what happened.

"And they passed through the Phrygian and Galatian region, having been forbidden by the Holy Spirit to speak the word in Asia; and when they had come to Mysia, they were trying to go into Bithynia, and the Spirit of Jesus did not permit them" (Acts 16:6–7).

Now wait a minute. They've had success, open doors, green lights. It's working. But when they move into the more central and southern regions, God closes the door. It's another of His surprises. Understand, there are people who don't know Christ in those parts of the country. There are many who may never hear of Christ. Nevertheless, God closes that door. So they think, *Obviously the Lord is leading us more toward the central and northern regions.* And so "when they had come to Mysia, they were trying to go into Bithynia."

Let's use our own geography to get a better sense of their journey. They start in South Carolina, make their way over into Tennessee, and there's a closed door. So they go down to Alabama, Mississippi, and Louisiana. "Maybe we can do it there." Nope, another closed door. " Well, let's go up to Kansas and on into Nebraska. How about North Dakota?" Slam, slam . . . closed door. One closed door after another.

No opportunity. They couldn't speak of Christ. In fact, it says, "the Spirit of Jesus did not permit them." And later, they were "forbidden by the Holy Spirit."

So they wound up at Troas. That's like trudging all the way to San Francisco. I mean, the next step, you get wet, okay? You walk right into the ocean. You can't go further than San Francisco. In Turkey, you can't go further than Troas. It's the northwesternmost point of the continent!

They went all the way to Troas. And as they looked at the Aegean, Paul must have thought, "Lord, what is this about?" He, Timothy, and Silas must have sought the Lord for hours, asking God, "What are You trying to do? What are You trying to tell us? I mean, look at the people we've left unevangelized. You've not allowed us to speak one word to them."

We don't know how long they were in Troas before the night vision appeared to Paul. I've been taught that the vision appeared their first night. But the narrative doesn't say that. Maybe they'd been there a week. Maybe they had been there a month, waiting and praying.

You see, because we like action, movement, it's our tendency to jump ahead to what happened. But pause and entertain the emotion of their disappointment. They couldn't preach in either Phrygia or Galatia, nor were they permitted to share Christ in Mysia or Bithynia. They had to pass by those populated places where the good news was sorely needed and come all the way to Troas. And apparently they weren't going to do much preaching there. It was a major city at that time. The harbor has now silted up quite a distance, leaving Troas inland today, but back then it was located at the sea. And some historians teach that it would have been the capital of the continent before too many more years. This is a significant metropolitan center . . . and they're not going to preach here? Paul and his companions must have been trying to figure out what God was saying.

You've been there, haven't you? This looked like what you ought to do, and you threw yourself into it, and you invested in it, whether it was time or money or gifts or effort, and . . . bang! . . . to your shock, the door slammed shut. It's often difficult to know why.

Sometimes it's to teach us an invaluable lesson. Several months ago I was speaking with a man who went through the lean years in Dallas. Like many through the 1970s and early 1980s, he had done well in the real estate market. I mean *really well.* Then, he said, "When it crashed, it was like you could hear the doors slamming. Banks under investigation suddenly called in their loans, and everything just dried up." This man said, "Back then, in the heyday of prosperity, I was driving a brand-new Porsche. Almost overnight I found myself driving a used, borrowed Chevy. One morning when I drove up to the tollway booth, I realized I didn't even have a quarter to put in the basket." From this enormous high to this closed-door low, the one-time high roller told me, "I lived in a bathrobe in my home for the better part of two years. Thankfully my wife was able to work and get us through it." The wide-open door suddenly slammed shut, leaving the man depressed for almost two years.

I don't know how long Paul was in Troas, but one night things changed. And aren't we grateful when there's a breakthrough. Isn't that a great moment? Imagine Paul's joy!

And a vision appeared to Paul in the night: A certain man of Macedonia was standing and appealing to him, and saying, "Come over to Macedonia and help us" (Acts 16:9).

But wait just a minute. Don't go any further. Stop right there. People read this and they think, *That's what I need, a night vision.* You don't. As I emphasized very early in this book, it's not dreams and visions we need in order to determine and follow God's will. If we didn't have a Bible, we would. If we didn't have the completed Scriptures, we would certainly need some phenomenal, Spirit-guided evidence that God wants us to do such-and-such.

As we discussed earlier, He has limited the revelation of His will to the pages of His Word. Look at it this way: When you exhaust the Scriptures, then you can start trusting in visions. But, obviously, no one can exhaust the inexhaustible Word of God. We have prayer, we have the Word of God, we have the Spirit of God dwelling within us, we have the counsel of wise friends, and with that, we have all we need. We don't need night visions. What we need most of all are scriptural insights and willing hearts.

But at that time Paul needed the Lord to reveal His plan visibly. And in this vision he saw "a certain man of Macedonia was standing and appealing to him, saying, 'Come over to Macedonia and help us.'"

Now if you don't know your geography, you can't appreciate what that call would require of Paul and his companions. They were in Troas, which is in westernmost Asia. Macedonia is all the way across the Aegean Sea, on the European side. And that man in Macedonia is saying, "Come over and help us." In other words, he invites them to another culture, another language, another continent. Closed door on one side. Open door on the other. And Paul was ready. Look at how he responded.

And when he had seen the vision, immediately we sought to go into Macedonia, concluding that God had called us to preach the gospel to them.

Therefore putting out to sea from Troas, we ran a straight course to Samothrace, and on the day following to Neapolis; and from there to Philippi, which is a leading city of the district of Macedonia, a Roman colony; and we were staying in this city for some days. And on the Sabbath day we went outside the gate to a riverside, where we were supposing that there would be a place of prayer; and we sat down and began speaking to the women who had assembled. And a certain woman named Lydia, from the city of Thyatira, a seller of purple fabrics, a worshiper of God, was listening; and the Lord opened her heart to respond to the things spoken by Paul. (Acts 16:10–14)

We aren't told many things. How long they tried the other regions, we're not told. How they responded when the doors closed, we're not told. How soon the vision came once they got to Troas, we're not told. We're not even told the identity of the man from Macedonia. But it doesn't matter who the person was. It was a vision miraculously sent from God. And the man said, "Come over." So they concluded that God had called them to preach the gospel over there, and immediately that's where they went.

This is the first work of evangelism in Europe recorded in the New Testament. This will mean the beginning of the church at Philippi, the church at Thessalonica, and the church at Corinth. God's at work. The door has now swung wide open. It had been closed, and now it's open. God did both without asking permission, without a warning, and without any explanation.

CLOSED AND OPEN DOORS STILL HAPPEN

Several years ago I was asked to speak at a reunion of the Navigators at Estes Park, Colorado. At the end of the week, one of the men drove me back to Denver so I could catch my plane. And on the way, he said, "Can I tell you my story?"

"Sure," I said.

"Actually, it's a story of closed doors and open doors."

"Great," I said, "I've had a few of those, so tell me what yours were."

"Well," he began, "my wife and I could not find peace, in any manner, staying in the States. And while at a conference years ago with a number of the leaders of the Navigators, I was offered the opportunity to open our work in Uganda.

"Uganda," he said. "I could hardly spell it when they pointed to me and said, 'Perhaps that's where the Lord would have you and your family go.'

"I went home, I told my wife and our children, and we began to pray." I believe he said they had three small kids at the time, and their oldest son was just about to start school. And he said to his wife, "Honey, are you ready to take on the challenge of Uganda?" And she said, "If that's the door God has opened for us, I'm ready for the challenge." Wonderful response.

So they flew to Nairobi, Kenya, where he put his family up in a hotel while he rented a Land Rover and drove across the border into the country of Uganda to check out the situation.

This was just after Idi Amin's reign of terror. My friend said, "One of the first things that caught my eye when I came into the village where I was going to spend my first night were several young kids with automatic weapons, shooting them off in the sky. As I drove by, they stared at me and pointed their guns." Nothing happened, but it was that kind of volatile setting. And he thought, *Lord, are You in this?* His heart sank as the sun began to set.

By now the streets were dark, and he pulled up at a little dimly lit hotel. Inside, he went up to the registration counter. The clerk, who spoke only a little English, told him there was one bed available. So he went up two flights of stairs and opened the door and turned on the light—a naked light bulb hanging over a table. He saw a room with two beds, one unmade and one still made up. And he realized, "I am sharing this room with somebody else."

That did it. He needed the kind of encouragement only God could provide. "I dropped to my knees and I said, 'Lord, look, I'm afraid. I'm in a country I don't know, in a culture that's totally unfamiliar. I have no idea who sleeps in that bed. Please, show me You're in this move!" And then, he said, "Just as I was finishing my prayer, the door opened and there stood this six-foot five-inch African frowning at me, saying in beautiful British English, 'What are you doing in my room?'"

"I stood there for a moment, and then I muttered, 'They gave me this bed, but I'll only be here one night.'"

"What are you doing in my country?" the African asked.

"Well, I'm with a little organization called the Navigators."

"Aahh! The Navigators!" And the African broke into this enormous grin, threw his arms around his new roommate, and laughed out loud.

"He lifted me up off the floor and just danced around with me."

"Praise God, praise God," said this African.

Finally they sat down at the table, and this brother in Christ, this African fellow Christian, said, "For two years I have prayed that God would send someone to me from this organization." And he pulled out a little Scripture memory-verse pack, and at the bottom of each of the verses it read, "The Navigators, Colorado Springs, Colorado."

"Are you from Colorado Springs, Colorado?" the African asked.

"I was," said the man. "But I'm coming to Uganda to begin a work for the Navigators in this country."

The door of new hope flew open in my friend's life. That African became a member of the man's board, helped him find a place to live, helped him rebuild a section of his home, taught him all about the culture, assisted him with the language, and became his best friend for the many years they were there, serving Christ . . . who "opens and no one will shut, and who shuts and no one opens."

Doors are closed. Doors are opened. Lives are changed.

FOUR GUIDELINES THAT WILL HELP

If you're still struggling with a closed door, I have four guidelines to share with you—guidelines that have helped me in my own process of dealing with the doors Christ has opened and closed.

1. *Since God is sovereign, He is in full control.* May I repeat that statement in Revelation 3? "I am the one who opens and no one shuts, I am the one who shuts and no one opens."

2. *Being in full control, God takes full responsibility for the results.* Don't try to carry that burden. It's not up to you to make the divine plan work; it's up to God. Your job is to walk in His will, regardless; it's God's job to make His will work.

3. *The closing of a good opportunity occurs in order to lead you to a better one.* Consider the story you just read. A good door closed in the States for that dear family; a better door opened in Uganda.

I've heard countless stories like this through my years of ministry. "I hit the closed door . . . I got to the end of my rope, I tied a knot and hung on . . . I trusted the Lord through this, and you can't believe what happened as a result of my not pushing my way in the direction I thought I was supposed to go." God took over and turned a jolt into joy.

4. *Not until we walk through the open door will we realize the necessity of the previously closed one.* As a result of obeying God, doing His will, accepting the closed doors, and walking through the open ones, God will honor you with a perspective you would never otherwise have.

Let me go back to my Uganda story. After more than a dozen years, the Navigator work was well established and the man's work there was finished. Another person from the staff of the Navigators came and picked up the work as my friend and his family returned to the States.

They had not been back quite a year, when his son's high school class went to Washington D.C. for their senior field trip. The father said to his boy before he left, "Son, here's forty dollars. I want you to buy something for yourself that will be a great memory for you of this trip to our nation's capitol."

So his son went to Washington, D.C., for several days. When he got back, he had a package with him. He said, "I want to surprise you, Dad." So the father waited until his son called him into his bedroom. As my friend walked into the room, he saw, hanging over the bed, a huge Ugandan flag. "This is what I bought with the money you gave me," said the boy. "Those years in Uganda were the best years of my life, Dad."

Talk about perspective. The man feared that by going to Uganda he might hurt or hinder his family, when, in fact, his son now had an abiding passion for God's work outside the borders of these United

States. It was a passion he would never have had if that man had not obeyed and walked through the open door.

God is full of surprises, isn't He?

Perhaps you've come to a closed door, and you've been resisting it, you've been pushing it, you've been fighting it. You've looked for someone to blame. You've determined that this is what you're supposed to be doing, and it's hard for you to accept the fact that the door is truly closed.

Accept it, give up the fight, let it be, my friend . . . let it be.

You've come to your own Bithynia or Phrygia, Galatia or Mysia, and to your surprise the door has closed. Ask the Lord to meet with you at your own personal Troas as you look out across that vast sea of possibilities. Ask Him to give you peace in a whole new direction. And be open, be willing. . . . be ready for a surprise!

It is easy to be disillusioned and discouraged and to think we have missed His will, when, in fact, we are in the very nucleus of that will. It is hard to have dreams dashed, to have hopes unfulfilled, to face a future that is unknown and unfamiliar and sometimes, if the truth were known, unwanted. But God has a way of guiding us unerringly into the path of righteousness for His name's sake.

Isn't it about time you stopped trying to figure it all out? Then let it be, my friend . . . let it be. You'll exchange a lot of intensity and worry for tranquility and relief. That's a pretty good trade, if you ask me. Or ask my friend who walked through that open door into Uganda.

12

A Better Way to Look at God's Will

Penetrating so many secrets, we cease to believe in the
unknowable. But there it sits nevertheless,
calmly licking its chops.

—H. L. MENCKEN, *Minority Report*

God's will alone matters, not my personal wants or needs.
When I played tennis, I never prayed for victory in a match.
I will not pray now to be cured.
—ARTHUR ASHE, *Former Professional Tennis Player*

Chapter Twelve

❦

A Better Way to Look at God's Will

As I have been saying since we started this journey together, God usually works His will in unexpected ways. Those ways are full of surprising twists and turns. But let me assure you of this: While none of us can guess the future, God is up to something great. And if we can ever figure it all out, it'll be terrific, right?

Well, don't get your hopes up. You never will. As we've repeated again and again, His decisions are unsearchable, and His ways are unfathomable, which brings us full circle to where we started: the mystery of God's will.

Recently I was in Israel, sitting on the southern steps of the temple in Jerusalem with our Insight for Living tour group while Steve Green sang "I Walked Today Where Jesus Walked." The thought crossed my mind, *Not only am I walking where He walked, I am walking with Him. As best I can tell, I am in the nucleus of God's plan for my life. Being in the center of where He has placed me, right here near the ancient wall of Zion, I'm contented.* (Who wouldn't feel that way, sitting there and listening to Steve's beautiful voice?)

But unlike that tour, where we knew every destination ahead of time, every hotel room, every lunch stop, I have no idea where this lifelong journey I am on with Him is going to take me. I really haven't a clue. The same is true for you, as a child of God. You have no way of knowing what you will experience even one minute from now. You don't know what lives you are impacting. You don't know where tomorrow will take you. You don't know the day of your death or how the Lord plans to call you home. All of this is part of His profound plan, His mysterious will. Only He knows all the details. The older I get, the more I like it that way.

At the moment, I am involved in a new church start-up north of Dallas in the once-farming community named Frisco . . . a town that is growing like Topsy. Now if anyone had told me a couple of years ago that I would be involved with a new church in Frisco, Texas, I would have responded, "Where's that?" But here I am, in the midst of another one of God's surprises! And two years ago I would have sworn that Insight for Living would be located in the Dallas area by now. Not so. Not yet. Maybe next year. Maybe never. Who knows?

I have two enduring goals in life. First and foremost, *I desire to learn how to think biblically.* I want to see life through the lens of God's eyes for the rest of my days. I don't want to argue with Him, I don't want to fight Him, I don't even need to understand Him, but I desperately desire to obey Him. And so I want to see life, whether it be struggle or joy, whether it be loss or gain, through God's perspective.

I want to be able to turn to the Scriptures and find direction and help. And when I can't find answers, I want to trust and to wait for God, even when I can't understand the reason behind where I'm going. And I want to have inner peace through all of that. . . . True contentment, like I felt sitting on those ancient steps of Jerusalem's temple.

And coming in a close second, *I want to encourage other people to do the same thing.* I want to help them know how to do what I am learning to do. That's why I'm writing this book.

I'm convinced that everything within us screams against that way of thinking and that way of living. From the time we were very small children, we have been self-centered. Our world revolves around what we want when we want it. And if someone else has it, we want it even more. And then when we get it, we want to keep it. But it doesn't satisfy, so we go looking for something else. Something more . . . always more. And so, unless something drastic takes place to change that ego-centric perspective, we spend our lives focused upon ourselves rather than upon God.

The result of all this is that we view God through human eyes. We think that He's really a lot like us, except He's older and He's stronger. We think His will is pretty much like our will, except His is smarter and has a longer view. We read our human style into God's character, so that when He throws us a curve, we view Him as unfair or untrustworthy. Or, worse, our faith gets shattered when bad things happen to people we admire. Or little children. Or whole countries.

For example, if I were God—which is a frightening thought in and of itself—I would never have allowed Dietrich Bonhoeffer to die at age thirty-nine in a concentration camp. I would have helped someone get rid of Hitler and then given Bonhoeffer at least fifty or sixty more years to live and to model, as well as to write more about the great life of faith.

If I were God, I would never have let Jim Elliott and those other fine young men be slain by the Auca Indians back in the mid-1950s. Never. I would have used them in ways that I considered worthwhile for many, many years.

If I were God, I would never have put Corrie ten Boom and her family through what they went through. Never. Because that's not fair to treat such godly people that way. I can think of some people I might put through that, but it wouldn't have been Corrie ten Boom, and it wouldn't have been Dietrich Bonhoeffer. It would have been people I felt deserved it, because that's the human way to do things . . . and so that's the way I think.

If I were God, I wouldn't have had Chuck Swindoll's mother die at age sixty-three, and I wouldn't have had his dad die a slow, painful death nine years later. I wouldn't have done it like that. My mother was fifteen years younger than my dad. She should have outlived him by fifteen years. I mean, that makes logical sense, doesn't it? Certainly from our perspective.

And if I were God, I wouldn't have had you go through the tough things you've gone through these last twelve months. You deserve better than that. Well, most of you anyway.

That may be sensible, logical, horizontal thinking . . . but that's not thinking biblically. That's putting God in human garb and giving Him our human emotions. That's calling fair what I consider fair, right what I consider right, wrong what I consider wrong. Only one major fly in this ointment: God cannot be put in our human framework. This brings us back to square one, which, again, is why I decided to write this book. There is a mystery, an aura, about the living God that is designed to force us to trust Him, even when we cannot figure Him out (which is most of the time). Why? Because, as we've learned in these chapters, He is inexplicable, He is unfathomable, He is infinite.

The mystery is purposeful, because His overall plan is profound. And let's not forget that His plan is not designed to make us comfortable; it's designed to make us more like Christ, to conform to His will. Nor is it intended to make human sense. In fact, more often than not, *God's will is downright humanly illogical.* There, I've said it.

In this life, we have focus choices. We can focus on ourselves, we can focus on our circumstances, we can focus on other people, or we can focus on God. When you think biblically (which is another way of saying theologically), you focus first on God. Regardless of what you want, regardless of the circumstances you're under (what are you doing under there anyway?), regardless of what others say or think, regardless of how you feel, God and God alone is working out His great plan. And in the final tally, it will be fabulous!

But wait. In the course of all this unfathomable mystery, we must not turn God into a cruel and unfair kind of peeved Deity. As I said, He has a divine purpose in mind. But that doesn't mean that He just carelessly tosses people into the winds of fate and then stands back with arms folded, thinking, *Ah, now let's see if they can make it through that.* God is not like that. As we've learned, He is full of tender mercies, faithful to the end, dripping with compassion.

As we discussed at the beginning of the book when we talked about Job and Jeremiah, we saw that even before the foundations of the world, He designed and put together the plan that would include the martyred missionaries, the Corrie ten Booms, the Dietrich Bonhoeffers, and millions of other names I could bring before you whose lives (and deaths!), in human terms, did not make sense.

That's a tough concept for us to grapple with, let alone grasp, because such knowledge is beyond our human way of reasoning. We never know anyone before they are born. We can't. We're finite. We do well to learn a little from history, looking back with 20/20 hindsight.

We take care of ourselves. We watch out for number one. We're focused far too much on how we look and what people are thinking and saying about us. If we have one button missing on our shirt or blouse, it's all we can do to exist until we can get alone and repair it.

Why? Because, bottom line, we don't think theologically. We think humanly. We're not nearly as concerned about what Scripture teaches as we are about what other people think and how they feel about us. If you and I genuinely believed the promises of God, we would not have worried this past week as we have worried. We would not have tried to shoulder that enormous load that is beyond our ability to carry. We would not have rationalized wrong or made up an excuse to cover our tracks. We would have flat-out told the truth and let the chips fall where they may. How very difficult it is to be totally and completely authentic!

Meanwhile, however, God is working His will in us. He is shaping us into the image of Christ, which means His Son's discipline, His endurance, His faithfulness, His purity, His attitude, His whole philosophy of life. God's goal is to make us like His dear Son. And that is a lifetime task . . . our lifetime, that is.

WHAT TO DO WITH THE UNEXPLAINABLE

It's a completely new way to look at God's will. Meaning? Do you know what I would suggest we do? Spend less time analyzing God and more time obeying Him. You say, "What are the practical ramifications of that?" That means this: When you follow His will and find yourself in a situation that you cannot explain, *don't even try.* If you do, you'll use human wisdom, and you'll just mess things up. Call it like it is. It's another of His mysterious surprises. Practice using words like "I don't know." "I don't understand." "This is beyond me." "It doesn't make sense to me . . . but that's okay. God knows."

Some young father has been diagnosed with a brain tumor. Why? I don't know. I cannot explain that. If I know that person, I want to comfort him and his family. I want to put my arms around them, and assure them of my prayers and love and confidence that nothing is a mistake with God. But that's the only answer I have. That's the limit of my understanding. And so I wait with them.

You and I could name things, specific things that we've gone through in the last several years, that make no logical sense whatsoever . . . but that's okay. We can't figure them out. But let me assure you, God is at work doing His mysterious plan (mysterious to us) which defies human logic. *So quit trying to make it humanly logical.* Trust Him. When we do, we begin the vital process of thinking biblically . . . thinking theologically.

Do you realize what a peaceful life you can live if you decide to live like this? Do you realize how relaxed you can be, how free of stress? Honestly. It is so helpful for me to remind myself: He is the One who is unfathomable. He is unsearchable. I'm neither.

So, how can we understand His ways? Face it, we cannot. That's precisely what Solomon wrote thousands of years ago:

Man's steps are ordained by the LORD,
How then can man understand his way? (Proverbs 20:24)

What a great line. How absolutely arrogant of us to think we could possibly understand the ways of the Almighty!

Job, in one of his many moments of struggle with the mysteries will of God, said,

> When He acts on the left, I cannot behold Him;
> He turns on the right, I cannot see Him. (Job 23:9)

"Lord, I am at a loss," said Job. Ever feel like that? I have . . . and very recently.

Cynthia and I were struggling for the longest time with a situation. I finally admitted to her, "I feel like the heavens are brass. It's like we can't get through." A little later she said to me, "I feel like we're just muttering words together here in our room." We prayed and waited and trusted and prayed some more. Nothing happened. We're still waiting. We still don't understand.

Have you ever felt that way? Job did. "I can't find Him," he admitted. "I look for Him and He's not around. If only He could just appear and I could reason my way through this, it would help so much." Sounds to me like Job's faith is getting a little thin. But then he says,

> "But He knows the way I take;
> When He has tried me, I shall come forth as gold. (Job 23:10)

Great, great insight! The overarching will of God is not about geography. (Where should I go?) It is not about occupation. (Where should I work?) It is not about exactly what car I should drive. (What color do you prefer?) The overarching, big-picutre will of God is not centered in the petty details of everyday life that we worry over. The will of God is primarily and ultimately concerned about our becoming like Christ. And in that sense, the will of God is a test. When He's tried us, and we have responded in obedience (even though we didn't understand why), we will come forth as gold.

"But I still don't understand," you say. "I don't understand why He's doing all this." Guess what? That's perfectly fine with Him. And so it's okay to admit it. It's all part of the gold-making.

Does it make the journey easy? It does not. Does it make it simple? It does not. Does it make everything that happens logical? You know that answer by now. Then what does knowing this do for you and me? It makes it bearable, especially when we call to mind that God makes no mistakes.

THINKING THEOLOGICALLY

We are riveted to earth, and we don't like things dangling. We don't even like dangling participles. We don't like dangling stories. Don't you hate it when the movie credits start to roll and you're still saying, "What? Wait a minute. Wait just a minute. I want to know who won. Who got the girl? What happened?" I hate that, when the movie just ends.

Well, a lot of things in life "just end." The credits roll before you get the final details figured out. You lost the romance that you thought was leading to marriage. It just ended. He or she just walked away from you. You lost a marriage that you thought God had put together forever. Our lives are full of stories like that—"a riddle wrapped in a mystery inside an enigma," to use a phrase coined by Sir Winston Churchill.

We don't know. And it's okay. See, it's the "okay" part that requires thinking theologically. It's also where the peace comes from, because we can relax as we leave it with God.

Which is another way of saying that we leave it with Romans 8. When things are dangling, when you can't figure out the ending and the credits are rolling, when things are not ending as you'd expected, it's time to turn to Romans 8. That works every time. I don't know what I would have done through much of my life if I hadn't had Romans 8 as my stabilizer.

When we think theologically, we find comfort in three things.

1. *We wait and persevere.* "But if we hope for what we do not see, with perseverance we wait eagerly for it" (Romans 8:25). Let that truth sink in. Read the verse once again. When we don't see what we had hoped to see, think theologically! Don't run. Don't panic. Don't doubt God's love. Don't fight. Wait and persevere.

When you get the results of your physical exam from the doctor, you wait, you persevere through it. You may get sick to your stomach, you may feel your head spin when the negative report comes, but you still wait. You persevere. Mentally, you connect with your Lord and express your willingness to trust Him entirely.

That takes faith. "Lord God, I don't know how to explain it. I don't know why this happened . . . why now, why me, why this? But I wait for You. I am determined, by Your grace and in Your strength, to persevere through this time. Because You make no mistakes, You don't have to explain it to me. I'm trusting in You right now." We risk trusting Him, not knowing how it's going to come out. He's trustworthy, so the "risk" is minimal!

2. *We face the test head-on but on our knees.*

And in the same way the Spirit also helps our weakness; for we do not know how to pray as we should, but the Spirit Himself intercedes for us with groanings too deep for words; and He who searches the hearts knows what the mind of the Spirit is, because He intercedes for the saints according to the will of God. (Romans 8:26–27)

You've been there, haven't you? "I just don't know how to pray about this." Of course . . . you and I have been there a hundred times. What happens? He tells us that "the Spirit Himself intercedes for us with groanings too deep for words." (We looked at this earlier, but it's worth a second glance.)

Oh, how we groan at times like this. Our soul is so troubled that we have no words to express our anguish. We fall to our knees, and, reading our inability to say what we're feeling, the Holy Spirit interprets our wordless mumblings and verbal stumblings as He intercedes for us. The Spirit intercedes as we groan on our knees: "I don't know why I lost my job, now of all times." "I don't know why I've been left to raise these four children on my own without the help of my partner." "I don't know why, Lord. All I can do is groan before You." And the Spirit intercedes for us, "according to the will of God."

To wait and persevere takes faith. Confident faith. To face the test head-on but on our knees takes humility. Submissive humility.

Humility says, "I'm willing to surrender." I'm willing to surrender my child. I'll weep as long as my grief lasts. I'm doing all I can to get the medical help we need. But ultimately, I am surrendering it all to You, dear Father. And if death comes, Lord, I accept it as part of Your plan."

This is serious stuff, folks. And I need to repeat myself, it works against our human nature to release anything. Everything in our flesh tempts us to clutch and cling. Remember? But here we humbly release as we face this test head-on . . . kneeling in full submission.

3. *We rest in our sovereign God and His plan.*

And we know that God causes all things to work together for good to those who love God, to those who are called according to His purpose. (Romans 8:28)

Sometimes I say out loud to myself, "This is for my good and for God's glory, even though I cannot begin to explain it."

Several weeks ago our youngest grandson, Jonathan, became very sick. As Cynthia and I were driving home from the hospital, I was thinking of that tiny, precious body lying there in his hospital crib . . . and I quietly said to Cynthia, "I think we're going to lose him." Those words got almost stuck in my throat . . . I could hardly get them out of my mouth. And then the next thing I said was, "Lord, I rest in You. You know what's best. You know the reason for this. You know how much we love that little boy. But he's Yours. He was Yours before he was ever his parents or ours." Cynthia and I wept as we drove the rest of the way home in silence. I turned Romans 8:28 over in my mind for the next several hours.

We rested in our sovereign God. We know that God causes "all things to work together for good" to those who love Him. Our little Jonathan is included in that. And let me add here, your situation is included in that, too.

In this situation, God graciously chose to bring healing. As I played with Jonathan yesterday afternoon, I gave Him thanks all over again. His tender *chesed* ministers to Cynthia and me in our sorrow and struggle.

I am learning that if you think theologically, you won't put a border around "all things." You'll let it be "all things." Your loss, your gain. Your prosperity, your bankruptcy. The accident, the fall, the loss, the disease, the disappointment. And yes, the relief, the success, the healing, the cure, the promotion. "All things work together for good . . . regardless. So we rest in our sovereign God. We rest in His plan, in what He considers best for us.

4. *We remember we're being conformed to the image of Christ.*

> For whom He foreknew, He also predestined to become conformed to the image of His Son, that He might be the first-born among many brethren. (Romans 8:29)

Waiting and persevering takes faith. *Confident faith.* Facing the test head-on but on our knees takes humility. *Submissive humility.* Resting in our sovereign God and His plan takes flexibility. *Unguarded flexibility.* And being conformed to the image of Christ takes sensitivity. *Willing sensitivity.*

"It's Your plan that's important, Lord, not my desire. I didn't bring myself into this world, and I can't take myself into heaven. Furthermore, I really don't know what is best for me or for those I love. That's Your call, Lord. Make me sensitive to the reality that You are in control, and You are using this—even this—to conform me to the image of Your Son. I want that most of all."

Together let's learn to think biblically—theologically.

I had a dear friend, who has now passed into glory, whom I loved and enjoyed being with. He was a classmate during our student years at Dallas Seminary. After he finished seminary, he and his wife and their firstborn child, a son, moved to Southern California, where my friend earned his doctorate. While they were there, they had two more children, two little girls. Then, one dark day, their little boy wandered into a neighbor's backyard, fell into their swimming pool, and drowned. On that tragic afternoon, they lost their adorable little boy.

My friend was grief stricken. This fine man of God got into his car and drove the freeways of Los Angeles for hours that night, screaming out to God about the loss of his boy. "And the things I said to God on the freeway," he later told me, "I would never repeat to another soul." Finally, hours later he pulled back into his own driveway, wet with sweat and tears, and turned his car off. He rested his head on his steering wheel and finally stopped sobbing. "It then dawned on me," he said, "that God could handle all of this. He could hear me, and He could understand where everything inside me was coming from. I finally came to terms with my loss . . . and grew closer to God than I'd ever been before." Ultimately, he found peace by forcing his mind to accept what occurred. He acknowledged that even the death of their little boy must be included among the *"all things"* in Romans 8:28.

That is thinking theologically.

If you counsel, counsel people theologically. If you advise, advise them theologically. If you're going through a trial, go through it theologically. Train your mind to acknowledge God's hand in *whatever* it is you're living with.

We've had enough humanistic reasoning. We've had enough of horizontal thinking. Let's just stop it and begin practicing words like, "I don't know," "I will trust," "I can't explain," "I release it all," because the star of the show is God. He is the beginning, He will be the ending, and in between, by His grace, He lets us be part of His perfect plan. . . . for His glory and for our good.

In the meantime, expect a mystery.

Conclusion

Here, we see through a glass darkly, but there face to face . . . There, riddles shall be unraveled, mysteries made plain, dark texts enlightened, hard providences made to appear wise. The meanest soul in heaven knows more of God than the greatest saint on earth . . . Not our mightiest divines understand so much of theology as the lambs of the flock of glory. Not the greatest master-minds of earth understand the millionth part of the mighty meanings which have been discovered by souls emancipated from clay.

—CHARLES HADDON SPURGEON, *Spurgeon's Gems*

＊

Conclusion

As you can tell, I'm standing in awe of mysteries these days. It's because they comprise so much of life.

Some are deeply serious. Others are lighthearted and humorous.

The washing-machine-in-our-laundry-room mystery comes to mind. Every family experiences it. You drop eight perfectly matched pairs of socks in the same load, only to pull out six matched pairs and a couple of individual socks that don't match anything. Not only do you not remember putting those two in . . . the others you did put in never show up again.

Then there's the mystery of traffic lanes. The one you find yourself in is invariably the slowest. Change lanes, and that one immediately slows to a crawl. Go figure.

Also, there's the peanut-butter-and-jelly sandwich mystery. Now, there's a tough one. Why, when accidentally dropped during the hand-held construction process, does it usually fall face down? (It has been suggested that whether it falls face down or face up is in direct proportion to the cost of the carpet.)

And how about the auto-trouble mystery? For three weeks you struggle with the same nagging problem with your car. So, early one morning you finally squeeze in time to run it by the shop. As soon as the mechanic lifts the hood, that baby purrs like a kitten. Not even the slightest miss in the engine. The guy in the overalls stares at you like *you're* the one needing to be fixed. You drive off puzzled—and halfway to work, it stalls on the freeway. Mysteries abound.

On a more serious note, there's the mystery of the sea, especially the tide, with its unusual marriage to the moon. Or the consistent, absolutely precise movement of the stellar spaces and the mind-stretching enormity of outer space. At the other extreme, a casual glance through a microscope reveals an otherwise invisible world buzzing with life.

And talk about tiny! Did you realize that if an electron could be increased to the size of an apple, and if a human being could be enlarged by the same proportion, a person could hold the entire solar system in the palm of his hand . . . and would have to use a magnifying glass in order to see it?

If you think those things are amazing, join me in trying to figure out what God is up to. We've spent twelve chapters together addressing this one. He gives; He takes. He starts; He stops. He grants us our desire; He abruptly says no. He surprises; He disappoints. He seems distant and uncaring; He surrounds us with His comforting presence.

He gives a dream, full of excitement and hope; He stops us short of fulfillment without one word of explanation. We lose.

On the other hand, we encounter a situation that appears hopeless, totally beyond our ability to handle . . . then He removes one obstacle after another, most of which we cannot explain, as we enjoy remarkable success. We win.

It's called God's inscrutable plan. I suggest it's time we stopped trying to unscrew it. Face it. It's beyond us. So? Deal with it. That's my advice, plain and simple.

Having walked with Him now for over fifty years, I've finally worked up the courage to say it publicly, loud and clear: God's will — from our finite, human standpoint—is a mystery. That's right, M-Y-S-T-E-R-Y.

Remind yourself of that two or three times a day. Before you know it, you'll really start to believe it and live it. When that happens, you cannot imagine how relaxed and relieved you'll be, filled with anticipation and adventure . . . for the rest of your life.

Endnotes

❧

Chapter One
A Process and a Puzzle

1. Elisabeth Elliot, *Keep a Quiet Heart* (Ann Arbor, Mich.: Vine Books, 1995), as quoted in *Christianity Today*, 6/14/99 issue, p. 84.

2. Origen, *On First Principles* (New York, N.Y.: Harper & Row, Publishers, 1966), n.p.

Chapter Two
God Decrees . . . God Permits

1. Grant Howard, *Knowing God's Will—and Doing It* (Grand Rapids, Mich.: Zondervan Publishing House, 1976), p. 14.

2. Ibid., pp. 14–15.

3. Garry Friesen with J. Robin Maxson, *Decision Making and the Will of God: A Biblical Alternative to the Traditional View* (Portland, Ore.: Multnomah Press, 1980), p. 244.

4. John R. W. Stott, *The Preacher's Portrait* (Grand Rapids, Mich.: William B. Eerdmans Publishing Co., 1961), pp. 11–13.

Chapter Three
Moving from Theory to Reality

1. Henry T. Blackaby and Claude V. King, *Experiencing God* (Nashville, Tenn.: Broadman & Holman Publishers, 1994), p. 44.
2. Ibid., p. 133.
3. Ibid., pp. 36 and 138.
4. Ibid., pp. 147–148.

Chapter Four
Fleshing Out the Will of God

1. Excerpts, as submitted from *The Knowledge of the Holy, The Attributes of God: Their Meaning in the Christian,* by A. W. Tozer, p. 111. Copyright © 1961 by Aiden Wilson Tozer. Copyright renewed. Reprinted by permission of HarperCollins Publishers, Inc.
2. Henry T. Blackaby and Claude V. King, *Experiencing God* (Nashville, Tenn.: Broadman & Holman Publishers, 1994), p. 38.
3. Footnote on Genesis 4:3–4, NIV *Study Bible,* (Grand Rapids, Mich.: Zondervan Publishing House, 1985), p. 11.
4. Stuart P. Garver, *Our Christian Heritage* (Hackensack, N.J.: Christ's Mission, 1973), p. 59.
5. Philip Schaff, *History of the Christian Church* (Grand Rapids, Mich.: William B. Eerdmans Publishing Co., 1910), p. 325.
6. As quoted by Harry Emerson Fosdick in *Great Voices of the Reformation* (New York, N.Y.: Random House, 1952), p. 8.
7. As quoted by Warren W. Wiersbe and David Wiersbe in *Making Sense of the Ministry* (Grand Rapids, Mich.: Baker Book House, 1983), p. 36.

8. Warren Wiersbe, *Walking with the Giants* (Grand Rapids, Mich.: Baker Book House, 1976), p. 61.
9. As quoted by Warren Wiersbe in *Walking with the Giants,* p. 61.

Chapter Five
Another Deep Mystery: God's Sovereignty

1. As quoted by A. W. Tozer in *The Knowledge of the Holy* (San Francisco, Calif.: Harper & Row, Publishers, 1961), p. 115.
2. Tozer, *The Knowledge of the Holy,* pp. 115–116. Used by permission.
3. Tozer, *The Knowledge of the Holy,* pp. 117–118. Used by permission.
4. John Oxenham, *Bees in Amber* (New York, N.Y.: American Tract Society, 1913), n.p.

Chapter Six
Reading God's Mysterious Lips

1. Walter Chalmers Smith, "Immortal, Invisible," (n.d.)
2. Eugene Peterson, *Run with the Horses.* Copyright © 1983 InterVarsity Christian Fellowship of the USA. Used by permission of InterVarsity Press, P. O. Box 1400, Downers Grove, Il 60515, and HarperCollins Publishers Ltd.
3. Peterson, *Run with the Horses.* Used by permission.
4. Ibid.

Chapter Seven
The Mysterious *Chesed* of God

1. As quoted by William Barclay in *The Letters to Timothy, Titus and Philemon* (Edinburgh, Scotland: The Saint Andrew Press, 1956, 1960), p. 53.

2. Barclay, *The Letters to Timothy, Titus and Philemon,* pp. 53–54.
3. Carolina Sandell Berg, "Day by Day," trans. Andrew L. Skoog (n.d.)
4. Francis A. Schaeffer, *No Little People* (Downers Grove, Ill.: InterVarsity Press, 1974), p. 112.

Chapter Eight
God's Mysterious Immutability

1. F. B. Meyer, *Christ in Isaiah* (Fort Washington, Penna.: Christian Literature Crusade; London: Morgan and Scott, [n.d.]), pp. 9–10.
2. David A. Redding, *Jesus Makes Me Laugh* (Grand Rapids, Mich.: Zondervan Publishing House, 1977), pp. 101–102.

Chapter Nine
Can God's Will Make Us Holy?

1. John White, *The Fight* (Downers Grove, Ill.: InterVarsity Press, 1976), pp. 179–180.
2. Paul Lee Tan, ThD, from "Gospel for the Youth," in *Encyclopedia of 7,700 Illustrations: Signs of the Times* (Chicago, Ill.: Assurance Publishers, 1979), p. 1404.

Chapter Ten
Surprised by God

1. A. W. Tozer, *The Root of the Righteous* (Camp Hill, Penna.: Christian Publications, 1955, 1986), p. 137.